Advanced Development with React

SSR and PWA with Next.js using React with advanced concepts

by

MEHUL MOHAN

FIRST EDITION 2020

Copyright © **BPB Publications, India**

ISBN: 978-93-89423-594

Distributors:

BPB PUBLICATIONS
20, Ansari Road, Darya Ganj
New Delhi-110002
Ph: 23254990/23254991

DECCAN AGENCIES
4-3-329, Bank Street,
Hyderabad-500195
Ph: 24756967/24756400

MICRO MEDIA
Shop No. 5, Mahendra Chambers,
150 DN Rd. Next to Capital Cinema,
V.T. (C.S.T.) Station, MUMBAI-400 001
Ph: 22078296/22078297

BPB BOOK CENTRE
376 Old Lajpat Rai Market,
Delhi-110006
Ph: 23861747

Published by Manish Jain for BPB Publications, 20 Ansari Road, Darya Ganj, New Delhi-110002 and Printed by him at Repro India Ltd, Mumbai

Dedicated to

My Family and Friends

My mom, dad, sister, and close friends, who have always believed in me.

About the Author

Mehul Mohan is an entrepreneur, developer and a security researcher. Currently, he is pursuing his bachelor's degree in CSE at BITS Pilani. He is a WWDC'19 Scholar and runs codedamn – a platform for people to learn coding. You'll often find him creating programming tutorials on his YouTube channel, codedamn, having over 100,000 subscribers. He has been acknowledged by companies such as Google, Microsoft, Sony, etc. for his contributions as a security researcher.

About the Reviewer

Self-motivated, charismatic programmer, currently working as Technology Analyst for Verizon, USA , focusing on Front-end programming. Involved in migrating Verizon's website pages from Angular to React Js.Holds degree in computer science from Mody University of Science and Technology, India.

A tech enthusiast and loves doing UI designing. Extensive experience in software development, front-end development in analysis, design, development and testing of web applications on OO JavaScript, HTML5, CSS3, BootStrap, ReactJS, JSON, Redux, JQuery. Known for high commitment, flexibility to juggle across multiple roles. Experience in contributing to Sprint Planning, Daily Scrum meeting, Sprint demo, and Sprint retrospective sessions. Extensive experiences in UI Development, Web UI analysis, Responsive design, coding, unit testing, implementation and support working with various projects.

Implementation in Agile Software Development Team using SCRUM, TDD (Test Driven Development). Expertise in developing applications using Core Java concepts like OOPS. Excellent communication and interpersonal skills, self-motivated, thrives on collaboration with people as a team player. Prior to Verizon, I have worked for Orange France as a Java developer. Was involved in migrating billing system of Orange to Java from DML(a legacy code language). Being a diploma holder in French language, the added knowledge of French also helped a lot for that project and used to take French classes for my colleagues, which was fun too.

Have also worked as an intern in HCL and C-DOT. Like to contribute to open source jobs online. Like to do freelance projects in free time. Hobbies: exploring new places around the globe, meeting new people and reading about space.

Acknowledgements

There are a few people I want to thank for the continued and ongoing support they have given me during the writing of this book. First and foremost, I would like to thank my mom – Mrs Ritu Mohan and my dad – Mr Vinay Kumar Mohan, for always being there when I needed them no matter what.

I would also like to thank my sister Mrs Ishumita Mohan, who also happens to be the technical editor for the book, for her constant support throughout.

Finally, I would like to thank Nrip Jain at BPB Publications for giving me this opportunity to write my first book for them.

Preface

With web evolving so rapidly in the past 5-6 years, it is a no-brainer to build on top of existing best practices available in the market instead of going through scratch. React is one such tool to build highly responsive and scalable web applications, and comes with best practices from industry, used by front faces of the internet like Facebook. Hence, it becomes extremely important for developers to level up their web development skills to include React as a skill in their toolkit.

With the increasing need of businesses to optimize for user experience as well as search engine optimizations, technologies like Server-Side Rendering (SSR) and Progressive Web Apps (PWAs) could enable companies to build better products whilst cutting down technical maintenance of existing codebase.

This book is a go-to handbook for developers who want to learn bleeding-edge React features, brush up their React skills, or start working with SSR/PWA using Next.js and React, which would eventually help them to scale their existing applications on the top of highly maintained and trusted open-source code. This book would take you through a journey of different discrete concepts you'll need to know in order to build parts of application ready for SSR deployment or converting it into a PWA. Over the course of 9 chapters in the book, you'll learn about the following.

Chapter 1 Introduces React to you. We'll dig up what React is and why it is a great choice for building highly scalable applications in today's world. We'll also quickly brush up some necessary JS concepts required for future chapters.

Chapter 2 Would cover setting up React using various methods and discuss the benefits and drawbacks of each. We'll also start writing basic applications with React and start seeing benefits React offers out of the box.

Chapter 3 Would introduce 2 ways to create components in React and discuss a modern approach React takes for components – functional way. We'll also work with hooks in this chapter and see why they make more sense than their counterpart – Classes.

Chapter 4 Introduces state management with React. Here we discuss possible options to manage the state with React. We'll see managing state with Redux, and using latest hooks – useContext and useReducer to emulate Redux store.

Chapter 5 Introduces server-side rendering in React, where we'll see what SSR is, and how it works. We'll implement SSR in this chapter ourselves from scratch, and discuss the pros and cons with it.

Chapter 6 This chapter introduces you to Next.js – a popular choice for SSR frameworks when doing SSR using React. We'll see how to setup Next.js and various baked-in features which come with it.

Chapter 7 We'll explore more advanced Next.js features in this chapter, digging deep into the framework and setting up API endpoints using Next.js framework.

Chapter 8 This chapter introduces Progressive Web Apps and how to create PWAs using Next.js and React framework.

Chapter 9 This chapter covers bleeding-edge React features and some information on how React works under the hood.

Downloading the code bundle and colored images:

Please follow the link to download the
Code Bundle and the *Colored Images* of the book:

https://rebrand.ly/5eino1r

Errata

We take immense pride in our work at BPB Publications and follow best practices to ensure the accuracy of our content to provide with an indulging reading experience to our subscribers. Our readers are our mirrors, and we use their inputs to reflect and improve upon human errors if any, occurred during the publishing processes involved. To let us maintain the quality and help us reach out to any readers who might be having difficulties due to any unforeseen errors, please write to us at :

errata@bpbonline.com

Your support, suggestions and feedbacks are highly appreciated by the BPB Publications' Family.

Table of Contents

CHAPTER 1

React 101

JavaScript: It is the programming language of the web. Since the dawn of the web, developers are eager to provide increasingly better experiences for the end-user in terms of interactivity, animations, effects, and stability. JavaScript made it all possible. As it progressed, there were needs for some obvious reasons to introduce frameworks and libraries, for faster development and better stability.

React is one such part of the ecosystem. React sells itself as "A JavaScript library for building user interfaces". But honestly, while being true to the statement, we think React goes much beyond that. It could be made into a complete ecosystem, powering some of the most complex web application systems, for example, Facebook.

We'll be quickly going through the React basics and then taking up intermediate to advanced topics, which would really give you the essence of React and eventually help you to start writing your production-ready applications with React.

Very simply speaking, React is a **User Interface (UI)** library. Let's break that down:

1. React, on its own says that it's a library, which means that it does not try to ship everything with it. Instead, you have the option to cherry-pick the things you want in your project and can implement them.

2. React says that it is a UI library, that is used for building interfaces visible to the user. What does that mean? In simple terms, it means creating and maintaining what the user sees on the screen.

Structure

- Introduction
- Understanding React
- Basic understanding of how React works as a UI library
- Declarative versus imperative programming
- Cheat-sheet for further React topics

Objectives

In this introductory chapter, we'll be understanding what exactly is React doing and why should one care. We'll be seeing on the surface, how it works as a UI library and how the declarative approach of React is so powerful in creating better UI systems. Finally, we'll want to get started with React programming, but would end the chapter with some notes that might be handy to see as a JavaScript refresher.

React is component-based

React makes use of *components*. The ideology is simple - React says that instead of coding everything at the same place (like we usually do while coding simple HTML pages), break different (and usually independent) parts of the page into different components. This increases the code maintainability by factors and allows developers to have faster and clean codebases. We'll have dedicated chapters on working with components, as it is the crux of React.

React is declarative

We'll focus mainly on two programming paradigms here -declarative programming and imperative programming. Let's start with a simple example.

When you write a code, you can specify:

1. What do you want to do?
2. How do you want to do?

If you specify both, you're making use of the imperative programming practice. If you're just specifying what you want to do, then you're using the declarative way of programming. Here's a simple example.

Consider that you want to draw a border around a box. In CSS, you'd simply say border: 2px solid black. This is declarative. You just said what you want to do, not how you want to do. On the other hand, if you try to draw the border in vanilla JavaScript, you have to specify four coordinates, and then draw the line manually using code. This would be an imperative way.

Declarative programming has its own pros and cons, but the pros almost always outweigh the cons:

1. Declarative code can make use of highly optimized algorithms. Since the "how" is abstracted from the end-user, the imperative model under declarative code can make use of seriously complex code to provide major performance boosts, while exposing an easy declarative way for users to use the same functionality at the same time.

2. Declarative programming brings other benefits like code scalability, reduced bugs, and more understandable code.

Coming back to React, it is **declarative**. This means that you just tell React "what" you want to do, and not "how" you want to do it. React, under the hood, manages everything for you in a very optimized way.

We will discuss on how the React virtual DOM, reconciliation and other optional advanced stuff works under the hood, in detail, in the last chapter.

Quick JS revision

Before we dive into the React ecosystem, we'd like to put some quick JS things that you should definitely be aware of, while working with React. Let's take a quick look at this section for now and come back later as you need.

this

this is surprisingly complicated for a lot of people in JavaScript. Keep in mind that in a function, this always refers to how that function is called, except for arrow functions, where this is lexically scoped:

```
function myName() {

  return this.myname

}
const myNameButArrow = () =>console.log(this.myname)
const person1 = { myname: "Mehul", myName }
const person2 = { myname: "James", myName }
const person3 = { myname: "Enzo", myName: myNameButArrow }
console.log(person1.myName())
console.log(person2.myName())
console.log(person3.myName())
```

The output is showcased in the following screenshot:

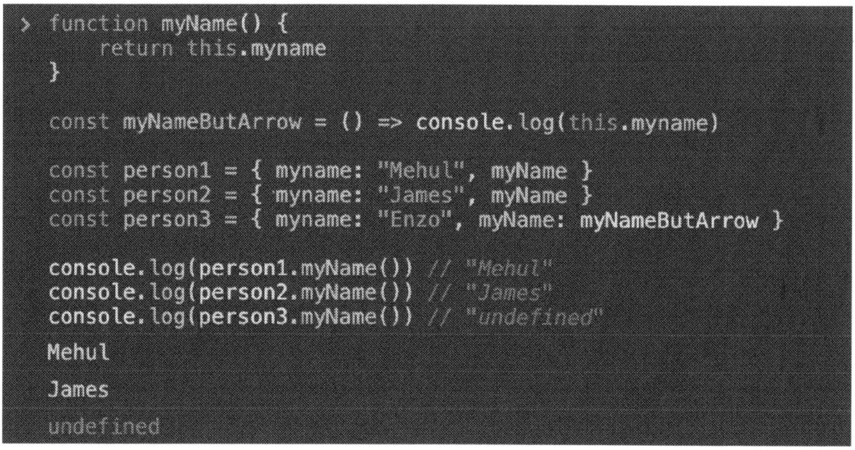

Figure 1.1: Output

Arrow functions

Arrow functions allow you to write smaller functions, lexical scoping to this, and cannot be instantiated with a new keyword:

```
const obj = {
myFunction: function() {

    return this

  },
coolFunction: () => {
```

```
    return this
  }
}
console.log(obj.myFunction()) // logs the original obj
console.log(obj.coolFunction()) // logs window (global object)
```

Here we see the same preceding code with its output as showcased below. As stated earlier, the first statement logs the original object, and the second statement logs the whole window object:

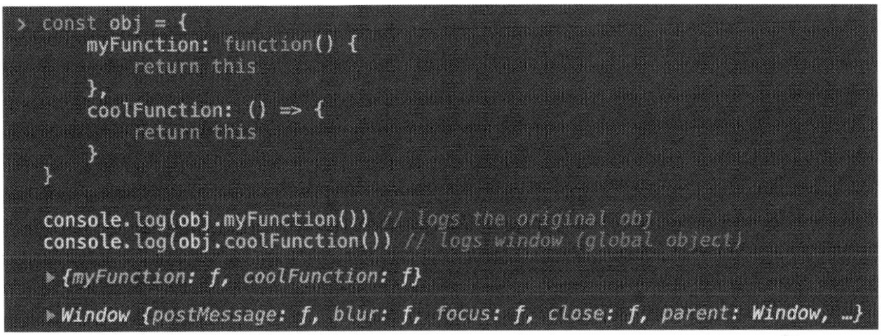

```
> const obj = {
      myFunction: function() {
          return this
      },
      coolFunction: () => {
          return this
      }
  }

  console.log(obj.myFunction()) // logs the original obj
  console.log(obj.coolFunction()) // logs window (global object)
  ▸ {myFunction: f, coolFunction: f}
  ▸ Window {postMessage: f, blur: f, focus: f, close: f, parent: Window, …}
```

Figure 1.2: Output

.map

`.map` allows you to manipulate an array without mutating the original array -that is, `.map` works on every element in an array and returns to you a new array, consisting of the elements you return from within the function passed in `.map`.

Here's a quick example of how maps would work in this case:

```
const arr = [{
  name: "Mehul Mohan",
  country: "India"
}, {
  name: "James Paul",
  country: "USA"
}]
const component = arr.map(name =>arr.name)
```

```
console.log(component)  //  logs  ["Mehul  Mohan",  "James
Paul"]
```

```
console.log(arr) // logs original object
```

The preceding code logs the changed array, as you would expect the map function to do. This, however, does not modify the original array.

.reduce

.reduce allows you to reduce the array to a single value.This is achieved with an accumulator, and the current value it is iterating over. Let's look at an example to understand:

```
x = [1,2,3,4,5]
```

```
x.reduce((acc, val) => acc + val, 0)
```

In the preceding example, reduce accepts a function thatis called every time with two values: the accumulator, and the current value. Whatever you return from the function, becomes the accumulator value for the next function call. Optionally, you can pass the initial accumulator value as the second argument to the .reduce function. This, if not present, would initialize the accumulator with the first element in the array, and would start reducing the array from the second value.

Classes

Classes in ES6 is merely syntactic sugar for functions. JavaScript is not OOP. It follows the prototypal inheritance model, and that's what classes do as well. Although, the proposed syntax makes it look very similar to OOP.

Here's an example of ES6 class:

```
class ILoveNumbers {
    constructor(num) {
this.anothernum = num
    }
getNum() {
console.log(this.anothernum)
```

```
        }
};
class IHateNumbers extends ILoveNumbers {
    constructor(num) {
        super(num**num)
this.num = num
    }
getNum() {
console.log(this.num)
    }
getNumFromParent() {
console.log(super.getNum())
    }
};
let obj = new IHateNumbers(5)
obj.getNum() // 5
obj.getNumFromParent() // 3125
```

Some important points to note aboutthe preceding code:

1. Here we created a simple class called `ILoveNumbers`, which just stores a number.

2. We created another class,`IHateNumbers,` which extends from our previous class. "`Extending`" in class-based syntax merely means that you're adding the parent class (function) to the prototypal chain of the current class (function).

3. We make use of a special keyword, called `super`. Using `super`, we can access the parent class. Remember, when using super in a method, super refers to the **prototype chain of the object** it was defined with. Thismeans, if I change the prototype chain of `IHateNumbers` to something else, the `super.getFav()` should not work as expected. Consider the following code:

    ```
    class C1{ method() { return 1 } }
    class C2 extends C1{ method() { return super.method()
    ```

```
} }
class C3{ method() { return 3 } }
class C4 extends C3{ method() { return 4 } }
const obj = new C4
console.log(obj.method()) // outputs 4
C4.prototype.method = C2.prototype.method
console.log(obj.method()) // outputs 1
```

4. Here you can clearly see that super.method() does not call the method of C3., Instead, it calls the method of C1. However, if you would have defined the method of C4 to return super.method(), it would call the method of C3.

Closures

Closure is a fundamental concept implemented in JavaScript that is extremely powerful and beautiful at the same time. To define closure in one line,:*the function remembers*. We have a common understanding as a Computer Scientist that when functions return, they remove all the local variable information associated with them. This is changed when you use a closure. For example, consider the following piece of code:

```
function a() {
  let value = 1
  return () => value++
}
const func = a()
func() // 1
func() // 2
func() // 3
```

In the preceding function, we can see that although value is a local variable, it is not destroyed when the execution of function a is completed. Instead, the function remembers.

More JavaScript topics

As you proceed through this book, you'll realize you would always need to use a lot more JavaScript than React as a framework itself. Although we've discussed some common JavaScript topics above, wesuggest reading more about the following ones, if you're interested in JavaScript's basic solidification and foundation. Since this is not a core JS book, we'll not be focusing a lot on the topics restricted to JavaScript, but you can always use this list to learn more:

1. Destructuring

2. Spread operator

3. ES6 import/export module syntax

4. Async/Await

5. Optional chaining in JavaScript

6. Nullish Coalescing

7. Prototypal inheritance model

8. Hoisting/variable scoping

Conclusion

This chapter covered some basic React concepts and fundamental JavaScript knowledge. In the next chapter, we'll be learning about how to set up our development environment with React and using it effectively. We'll be exploring React basics and make our way up to server-side rendering framework Next.js, and cover information about Progressive Web Apps eventually. Hold tight for a code-train ride!

CHAPTER 2

Setting up React

In this chapter, we'll see some common, and not so common ways to set up React into your development workflow. We'll start from the very basics, of which editor you should probably go with, all the way to the best way for you to bootstrap your React application, so that it matches your needs and is convenient for you to take it to the production. Let's go!

Some people like to work with **Integrated Development Environments** (**IDEs**) all the time. We'll take a different approach here. IDEs tend to get super heavy for things like web development. Plus, IDEs abstract a lot of stuff, so you get to learn a lot less than you expect. We'll be using (and learning) command line, working with code using light text editors and build great applications! Let's proceed with the chapter.

Structure

- Choosing a text editor
- Setting up Node and NPM
- Ways to set up a React project
- Hello World with React
- JSX
- Shifting to TypeScript for React

Objective

We'll start this chapter with a simple choice—choosing a text editor that you would like to write the code in. We'll then be moving on the installation and setting up of the required technologies, which would help us explore the ways to set up our first react project. We'll also be exploring what JSX is and how it works. Finally, we'll shift our focus to TypeScript for React and stick with it throughout the book, for a better type system and bug-free code.

Choosing a text editor

First things first -you need a place to write code. Here's a list of text editors that we recommend personally.

#1 – VSCode

This is the most popular text editor out right now and a major chunk of web developers you find, would be using VSCode all the time. VSCode is fully customizable, with tons of additional plugins to supercharge your productivity. It is cross-platform (macOS/Linux/ Windows) and you can get a stable binary for your platform here: https://code.visualstudio.com/#alt-downloads.

#2 – Sublime Text

Another great text editor is Sublime Text. If you're unhappy with VSCode, Sublime text can be the second choice. You can purchase it, but you're not forced to. Sublime Text allows you to use it for free for a very long time, with a little popup coming to your screen every week or so to upgrade. It also ships with a powerful package system and great themes. Download it from here: https://www.sublimetext. com/3.

#3 – Atom

Atom is also a decent alternative, if you're looking for text editors. It does include a package manager, is fully customizable and free! You can download the Atom text editor from here: https://atom.io/.

Setting up nNode and NPM

Once your text editor is installed and is ready (which should relatively take 5-10 minutes), it's time to setup node and npm. If you already have that on your system, you can skip this section. Node is basically taking the JavaScript engine (a piece of code responsible for running your written JavaScript on the machine) and putting it on your computer as a local app, instead of embedding it inside just a web browser. And npm, is its package manager to add and remove the packages and dependencies.

Windows

For Windows, follow the steps to install the latest stable versions of node and npm:

1. Go to https://nodejs.org/en/download/.

2. Download the **Windows Installer (.msi)** file. Choose according to your operating system - 32 bit or 64 bit.

3. Follow the wizard instructions and complete the installation.

4. Verify your installation by opening `cmd` from the **Start** menu.

5. Type `node -v` in cmd and check if it displays a number.

Linux

For Linux, follow the steps to install the latest stable versions of node and npm:

1. Open your command line (terminal).

2. Write `sudo apt-get update &&sudo apt-get install npm`.

3. Depending on your distribution, you might not have apt-get as the package manager. Just find out what your package manager is, and install the `npm` package from the official repository.

4. Once it completes, write the following: `sudonpm install -g n`.

5. This will install a node version manager package called n on your systems

6. Once this completes, write: `sudo n stable`.

7. This would finally install a stable release of both, node and npm, and add it to your path as well.

8. Finally, quit your terminal and start again. This time write `node -v`, and see a version number pop up. You're good to go now!

macOS

If you have a macOS system, here are the steps you need to follow in order to get node and npm on your systems:

1. On macOS, you need a brew package manager. If you don't know what it is, you probably don't have that installed. Write the following in your command line to install the brew package manager: `/usr/bin/ruby -e "$(curl -fsSL https://raw.githubusercontent.com/Homebrew/install/master/install)"`.

2. You can find the brew installation instructions here as well: https://brew.sh.

3. Once the brew is installed, write `brew install node`.

4. Wait for it to install.

5. You're done!

Setting up React projects

Now, let us discuss of the various ways in which we could bootstrap our React project. We'll start with the most barebones method first, and gradually proceed towards more advanced methods.

#1 – Setting up with CDN

This is the most straightforward way to write Hello World in React. You just throw in the React libraries using some CDN website, and you're good to go. For example, consider the following code:

```
<!doctype HTML>

<html>
```

```
<head>
<title>React hello world</title>
</head>
<body>
<div id="root"></div>
<script src="https://unpkg.com/react@16/umd/react.
production.min.js"></script>
<script src="https://unpkg.com/react-dom@16/umd/react-dom.
production.min.js"></script>
<script src="https://unpkg.com/babel-standalone@6/babel.
min.js"></script>

<script type="text/babel">
    class HelloWorld extends React.Component {
render() {
            return (<p>Hello world</p>);
        }
    }
ReactDOM.render(
<HelloWorld />,
document.getElementById('root')
    );
</script>
</body>
```

A lot is happening in this code. Let us break this down quickly:

1. Firstly, we're loading two scripts—react itself and react-dom. Why 2? Well, as you can see that React itself isn't just limited to the web. You see React being used on mobile phones as well using React Native. That means React is independent of the **Document Object Model** (**DOM**), a construction which the browser uses to render HTML. Because we're working with web pages, we need the core library, that is, React, plus we need the reconciler that would glue React and DOM (browser) together, hence React DOM.

2. Then we load a library called **babel** (more on this in next points).

3. Finally, you can see that we create a script tag with the type `text/babel`. This is because we're not going to write pure JavaScript in this script tag. We'll write some code that needs to be pre-processed, before being executed as regular JavaScript.

4. Finally, we see some React constructs (classes and ReactDOM), but we'll ignore it for now. What is interesting is that we wrote `<p>Hello World</p>` directly, without any quotes. This is not an error. It is, in fact, JSX (more on this will follow).

#2 – Using create-react-app

`create-react-app` is a tool that allows very quick bootstrapping of React projects with minimal configuration to be done by the end-user. To use it:

1. Open your terminal again (cmd on Windows or Terminal on macOS/Linux).

2. Write `npm install create-react-app -g`.

3. Once that is completed, write `create-react-app hello-world`.

4. Let it complete. Once it does, you'll see a directory named `hello-world`. `cd hello-world` and write `npm start`.

5. This will start your local development server. Open the folder in your favorite text editor, and a browser window would open automatically. There onwards, you can make your changes and see them reflecting directly in the browser.

#3 – Setting up from scratch

This is a bit advanced for starting with React but setting this up means that you are fine-tuning and controlling every aspect of your React application. We'll follow a model like create-react-app, but this time all the configuration files and folders would be visible to us:

1. Create a new folder called `hello-world-scratch`:

    ```
    cd hello-world-scratch
    ```

2. Then do a `npminit -y`, which would create a `package.json` file in that directory. This file is responsible for handling your project dependencies.

3. Then do `npm install react react-dom –save`.

4. This will install react and react DOM libraries (just like we discussed above) and would mark them as *"need-at-production"* dependencies (that is, we'll need React and ReactDOM even when we're shipping the application).

5. Finally, do `npm install webpack webpack-dev-server webpack-cli @babel/core babel-loader @babel/preset-env @babel/preset-react html-webpack-plugin --save-dev`.

6. This will install all the `devDependencies`, the dependencies you need while coding the application, but not on production. We'll breakdown the need for these dependencies now:

    • **Webpack**: Webpack is a module bundler system. Simply speaking, it combines various assets of yours (JS, CSS, and so on), so that you can freely write your code in a maintainable way (i.e. clean and different files) and could later automate the combination and compression of the code.

    • `webpack-cli` enables webpack to perform this.

    • `webpack-dev-server` enables us to launch a server to see the output of the code.

    • `html-webpack-plugin` would allow us to dynamically generate an HTML page for react scripts to work on. Don't worry, we'll be mostly working with JavaScript files, so we don't need to statically create HTML files anyway.

    • `@babel` packages run the JSX transformations into normal, executable JavaScript code (more on JSX below).

7. Once you do that, in your project directory in the command line, do touch `.babelrc`.

8. It'll create a dotfile called `.babelrc` (notice the dot at the front of the filename).

9. Paste the following content inside it: { "presets": ["@babel/preset-env", "@babel/preset-react"] }.

10. This tells babel to use the following presets, before working on the React code. Simply speaking, it loads a bunch of pre-defined rules to babel about how it should handle JSX.

11. Finally, because webpack is the main bundler of our project, we need to tell the webpack to let babel handle the steering wheel on the appropriate files. Here's how we do that:

- Create a file called `webpack.config.js` in your project's root, and write the following in it:

```
const path = require('path');

const HtmlWebpackPlugin = require('html-webpack-plugin');


module.exports = {
    entry: path.join(__dirname, 'src/index.js'),
    output: {
        path: path.join(__dirname, 'bundle'),
        filename: 'bundle.js'
    },
    module: {
        rules: [
            {
                test: /\.(js|jsx)$/,
                exclude: /node_modules/,
                use: ['babel-loader']
            }
        ]
    },
    mode: process.env.NODE_ENV || 'development',
    resolve: {
        extensions: ['*', '.js', '.jsx']
    },
    devServer: {
```

```
contentBase: path.join(__dirname, 'src')
    },
    plugins: [new HtmlWebpackPlugin({
        template: path.join(__dirname, 'src/
index.html')
    })]
};
```

- This simply tells the webpack that hey webpack, load babel whenever you're processing a `.js` or `.jsx` file.

- We need to launch a webpack dev server when we want to see the output, so we'll add this to the `scripts` key to the `package.json` file:`"start"`: `"webpack-dev-server --open"`.

- Now we'll create a static HTML file for this, to use in `src/index.html`:

```html
<!DOCTYPE html>
<html lang="en">
<head>
<meta charset="UTF-8">
<meta name="viewport" content="width=device-width, initial-scale=1.0">
<meta http-equiv="X-UA-Compatible" content="ie=edge">
<title>React Hello World!</title>
</head>
<body>
<div id="root"></div>
</body>
</html>
```

- Finally, let's touch `src/index.js` and write the following in it:

```
import React from 'react'
import ReactDOM from 'react-dom'
```

```
ReactDOM.render(<div>Hello World</div>, document.
getElementById('root'))
```

- That's it! Now go ahead and run npm start in your project's root directory. Your web browser should open, and Hello World should appear on your screen.

For this course, however, we'll be making use of `create-react-app` approach as it abstracts away all the webpack and babel configuration and gives us a great opportunity to write and focus on our React code.

JSX

Let's dive a little into JSX, the weird HTML syntax that we just wrote in JavaScript file:

```
ReactDOM.render(<div>Hello World</div>, document.
getElementById('root'))
```

Do you see what we did there? You can see a div tag written directly, without the quotes. That is JSX. JSX stands for JavaScript eXtensible markup language.

JSX is a different syntax. It allows you to harness the simplicity of the HTML markup, whilst making powerful JavaScript computation together. You can include JavaScript expressions, dynamic props (properties, or what we call attributes in regular HTML), and handling UI and functionality at the same time.

You could also write expressions in JSX using curly braces. Consider the following JSX example:

```
const elem = <div>Hello World { document.location.href } {
5 + 5 } { `Regular string` } </div>
```

This is a completely valid JSX syntax, but definitely not valid JavaScript. So, what happens under the hood?

JSX transformation

React compiles down JSX to normal ES5 code. Consider the following example:

```
const elem = <div className="a-classy-div">JSX seems so
cool!</div>
```

This example is compiled to the following:

```
const elem = React.createElement('div', { className:
'a-classy-div', 'JSX seems so cool!' })
```

The latter definitely looks like a valid JavaScript syntax. This is the magic of JSX. You get a visual aid of writing the React components, because now you can easily avoid the cumbersome, additional JavaScript code that you have to write for the UI part.

In fact, the preceding two code snippets are the same, which means that instead of JSX you could directly write that `React.createElement` part. But of course, JSX is much cleaner to eyes than the barebones JS, for UI development.

Moving to TypeScript

Now that we're up and running with a basic JavaScript project in React, it's time to introduce TypeScript. We'll not be focusing too much TypeScript with all the typecasts and interfaces and everything baked into, right away. Rather, we'll just use the best parts of TypeScript (that is, auto completion and error-free code practices) and would use it throughout the book. Here's how you're going to start a TypeScript project:

- Nuke the JS hello world folder we created earlier.

- Assuming that you've already installed the create-react-app utility using the instructions above, in your command line, write `create-react-app hello-world-ts –typescript`.

- This will initialize your React project with TypeScript.

- Here's how your final file structure should look like:

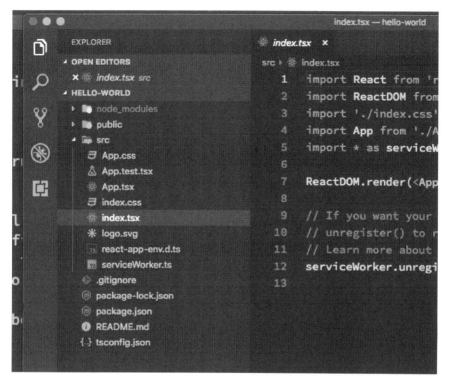

Figure 2.1: File structure

Finally, we're ready to work with React!

Conclusion

We learned what JSX is, how to create our project with React, and eventually, move to TypeScript, as it provides better type checking and allows you to write bug-free code more easily. In the further chapters, we'll be diving deep into React and seeing the fundamentals, as well as the core concepts associated with it.

CHAPTER 3

Components

Components area fundamental part of React. The ideology goes like this: everything on a webpage can be broken into reusable views called components. These components can be linked with each other, could be completely independent, could be aware oftheir parent components or might as well be completely *"dumb"* to their environment.

Let's see more abouthow to work with them.

Structure

- About components
- Class versus functional components
- Functional components
    - Props
    - Children
    - Hooks
        ▸ useState
        ▸ useEffect
        ▸ useCallback
    - Custom Hooks
- Class components
    - Props

- State
- Lifecycle methods
  - ▶ getDerivedStateFromProps
  - ▶ Render
  - ▶ getSnapshotBeforeUpdate
  - ▶ componentDidMount
  - ▶ componentDidUpdate
- Conclusion

Objectives

This chapter aims to introduce you to components in React and the two major ways to create them. We'll start with functional components and soon would realize that it is a much better and cleaner way to create components compared to the class-based approach tocreating components. We'll learn some edge cases and eventually, learn about hooks and lifecycle events in functional and class-based components, respectively. We'll finally conclude the chapter with clarity of components in mind moving towards more advanced concepts.

About components

Components are the heart of React. Think of components as pieces of code which are decoupled from the main big JavaScript bundle to provide maintainability and makes it easy to add features on top of the existing codebase. Usually, you'd want to separate components on the basis of where and how they appear in the UI of the page. With React 16.8 and above, there are precisely two ways to write components with similar functionality as we're going to see now— functional components and class-based components.

Class versus functional components

Class-based components have been present in React fora very long time. In fact, almost forever, it has been the only way to create a working React component with its own state. This was changed with the introduction of hooks, which we'll look at in the next section. However, here are a couple of points about class and functional components after hooks:

1. Functional component (after hooks) is clearly a better way to create components in React because they're much cleaner than classes, avoids a lot of common pitfalls you'll see in class-based components code (example - binding of this), avoids mutation of state and uses side effects instead of lifecycle-based model.

2. React core team recommends preferring hooks as well because of the reasons stated above. Although class-based components are not going anywhere anytime soon, still, we could all agree that functional components arethe future React libraryis aiming at.

With that being said, there's always an advantage inlearning more than you'd use. We'll cover class-based components here quickly and dive deep into functional components which is a more important aspect now. But first, let's start with functional components.

Functional Components

Functional components have existed in React for a long time. Let us take a look at this hello world React code before going further:

```
import React from 'react'

import ReactDOM from 'react-dom'

function App() {

    return <p>Hello World</p>

}

ReactDOM.render(<App />, document.getElementById('root'))
```

You can see here, that we're using a function called App here as a React component. Well, how does one know that it is a React component? When you use it as JSX (like <App />), it gets transpiled to the following:

```
import React from 'react';

import ReactDOM from 'react-dom';

function App() {

  return React.createElement("p", null, "Hello World");

}
```

```
ReactDOM.render(React.createElement(App, null), document.
getElementById('root'));
```

So what is happening here?

1. Everything you write in JSX is transpiled to equivalent React calls (we discussed this in Chapter 1) JSX is just syntactic sugar for the preceding example.

2. React.createElement returns a JavaScript object which looks something like this:

```
> React.createElement('div', null, 'Hello World')
<- ▼{$$typeof: Symbol(react.element), type: "div",
     $$typeof: Symbol(react.element)
     key: null
   ▼props:
       children: "Hello World"
     ▶__proto__: Object
     ref: null
     type: "div"
     _owner: null
   ▶__proto__: Object
```

Figure 3.1

Now, we don't want to get into the internals of React right now, but eventually, React uses this object to create a tree, a virtual DOM, to say. Let's get back to some properties of the functional components now.

Props

Passing props (short for properties) is a common scenario, and you'll be doing it almost always as a way to pass down data to child components. React works in a way where parents pass down data to child components. Sure, with the context API you could magically transport the data multiple level downs (more on this later), but props enable you the simplest way of data passing. Let's take a look at this example:

```
interface props {
```

```
    name: string

}


const App: React.FC<props> = props => {

    return <p>Hello {props.name}</p>

}
ReactDOM.render(<App name="Mehul" />, document.getElementById('root'))
```

Here you can see that we're making use of TypeScript to enhance React. Instead of creating a function using the function keyword, we're making use of the arrow function notation because right now, you cannot have typed functions.

React.FC or React.FunctionalComponent types (TypeScript) the App component which could accept and validate what props goes to the component when using the component. Additionally, you could list all the props and their data types in the interface as defined.

Children

A special prop called children is available for React components which basically includes anything passed within an opening and closing tag of your custom component. Now, I mention anything passed instead of a component passed because you could literally pass anything you like - a component, a string, a function, and so on. Take a look at the following example:

```
const App: React.FC<{ name: string }> = props => {

    return <div>

    Hello {props.name}
<div className="children">

        {props.children}

</div>

</div>

}
```

And we could call this component as:

```
<App name="Mehul">
```

```
<p>Hey there!</p>
```

```
</App>
```

That is one way of using the children prop. Another way you could use them is via a function. See this example:

```
const App: React.FC<{ name: string, children(one: string, two: string): JSX.Element }> = props => {

  return <div>

    Hello {props.name}
<div className="children">

      {props.children('one', 'two')}
</div>

</div>

}
```

And that's how we'll use this component:

```
<App name="Mehul">

  {(one: string, two: string) =><p>Hey there! Passed attributes: { one } { two }</p>}
</App>
```

Here's a quick summary of what we did in the last example:

1. We created our custom children type receiving two string parameters which return a JSX.Element (that is, that <p> tag).

2. In the component, we used props.children as a function and called it (instead of simply rendering it) with two values passed.

3. The parent renders the child component with the values passed by the child to the parent. This is a neat trick to pass a little bit of data from child to parent;usually, data is passed from parents to children but this way you could achieve the opposite.

In fact, what we did previouslyis called as **render props** method. It simply refers todata passing when a prop (children in our case) is a function instead of a JSX element or a regular value.

Hooks

Before React 16.8, it was not possible to create stateful functional components just using functions. You see where the problem lies unless, like class components, there was no way to make use of any *state* object. But this was changed with the introduction of hooks. Introducing state with hooks could bring in tons of benefits. Functional components could now *remember* their context. Let us start with the various kinds of useful hooks we have now in React and how to use them.

useState

useState hook allows you to bring this.state and this.setState functionality from classes to functional components. Here's a quick example on how to use them:

```
function App() {

const [name, setName] = useState('Mehul')

  return <p>Hello {name}</p>

}
```

Let's focus on this line const [name, setName] = useState('Mehul'). The useState method returns an array with two elements, the first being the getter and second being the setter. If you just call console. log(useState("Mehul")) within your functional component you're going to see something like this:

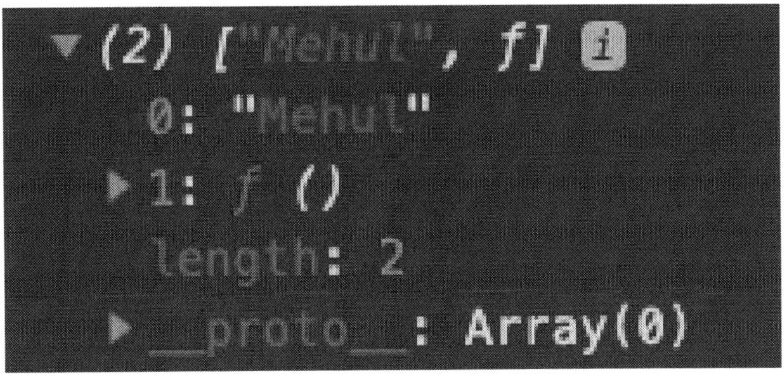

Figure 3.2

Here, we can clearly see the array having the first value as the getter and the second value as a function. This function, when called, will update our setter variable, similar to how calling this.setState does that. Let's take a look at this simple example:

```
function App() {

const [name, setName] = useState('Mehul')

  setTimeout(() => {

    setName(Math.random())

  }, 1000)

  return <p>Hello {name}</p>

}
```

Here, when you run this code, you'll see that the name changes every second to a random number between 0 and 1. Note that it is a convention to use X and setX for the variable names of getter and setter. You can, however, use whatever you like, but I'd recommend sticking to the convention as it makes it easy to distinguish.

useState is not synchronous

That means, whenever you call useState, thereis no guarantee that after calling it if you use the getter you'll get the updated value. For instance, consider this example:

```
const App: React.FC = props => {

const [currentNumber, setCurrentNumber] = useState(Math.random())

  function changeState() {

setCurrentNumber(Math.random())

    console.log(`New number => ${currentNumber}`)

  }

  return <button onClick={changeState}>Click Me { currentNumber }</button>

}
```

Here's the output of the code:

Figure 3.3

If you use this component, you'll see that what you see in console isn't what is reflected in the UI. This is because useState runs asynchronously and wouldn't update the variables right away.

There's another problem now if setX is not asynchronous, that means if the next state of the variable depends on the previous state, we cannot use the X directly inside setX! Fortunately, for that, react allows you to pass a function inside setX whose first argument is guaranteed to be the new value. Let's see this example to learn more:

```
const App: React.FC = props => {
const [counter, setCounter] = useState(0)
  function add() {
setCounter(counter => counter + 1)
  }
  function sub() {
setCounter(counter => counter - 1)
  }
  return <>
<p>{ counter }</p>
<button onClick={add}>++</button>
<button onClick={sub}>--</button>
```

```
</>
}
```

Couple of things to be noted here:

1. We could use nameless JSX element (simply <> and </>) - This would not show in the DOM structure.

2. We could pass a function inside setX instead of the updated value. If you pass a function, React would call that function with the latest state variable value and then whatever that function returns would be assigned as the latest state.

A general rule of thumb is if your state mutation involves results based on the previous state, use the functional parameter approach;otherwise you could directly pass the new value.

useStatecallback

Well, in class-based components, we had a callback associated with this.setState which could be used in case you wanted to wait for the state variables to update and then trigger an action. It is not that straightforward with hooks, however, you could make use of another hook to achieve the same effect. Let's take a look at that hook now.

useEffect

This hook allows you to call a piece of code whenever something *changes*. Think of useEffect as a custom watch implementation over React's inbuilt infrastructure.

Here's a very simple example of useEffect:

```
const App: React.FC = props => {
const [counter, setCounter] = useState(0)
  useEffect(() => {
    document.title = 'Counter is at ' + counter
  })
  return <>
<p>{ counter }</p>
<button onClick={() =>setCounter(c => c + 1)}>Increment</button>
```

```
</>
}
```

Alright, here we could see that we're making use of the useEffect hook by passing a function to it. This function is executed every time React renders (or re-renders) our component. This function eventually sets the document's title to our counter value. And in the function, you'll always have the latest value of the state variable. This is because React does not mutate the state variables at all! When using functional components and hooks, React does not mutate state ever. You could see this fairly clearly by the use of our const keyword over simple string/number values too. Instead, whenever React re-renders our component, the useState() function returns the newly updated state to the state variable, and the useEffect function calls the passed function on every single render.

useEffect dependencies

You could quickly see how useEffect could become a little heavy on performance as it would be running our passed function again and again on every render even when nothing has been changed. Let's take a look at the following example:

```
const [counter1, setCounter1] = useState(0)

const [counter2, setCounter2] = useState(0)

  useEffect(() => {

    document.title = 'Counter is at ' + counter1

    console.log('Effect called')

  })

  return <>
<span>{ counter1 }</span> 

<span>{ counter2 }</span>

<button onClick={() => setCounter1(c => c + 1)}>Increment Counter 1</button>

<button onClick={() => setCounter2(c => c + 1)}>Increment Counter 2</button>

</>
```

And the output associated with the code above:

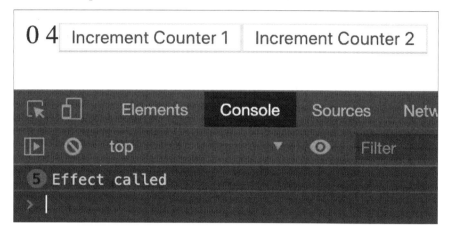

Figure 3.4

Clearly, we never updated counter1, but still, React calls our useEffect function on every re-render. We can do better. We can tell React that a particular effect only uses a certain set of variables passed as an array, which if changed, React should call the effect function again. Otherwise, it's just no point (because the value is the same for our state variables anyway). To do that, we can pass a second argument to the useEffect hook, which would be our dependencies for that effect. Let's take a look at the same example again but this time with added counter1 as a dependency:

```
useEffect(() => {
    document.title = 'Counter is at ' + counter1
    console.log('Effect called')
}, [counter1])
```

And the output associated now is:

Figure 3.5

You see, now we get **Effect called** only once because effects run initially after the first render. Other than that, as long as counter1 is untouched, the effect function won't run.

useEffectcleanup

The hook useEffect provides you with an option to clean up any subscription you want to get rid of before either the component is unmounted or it is re-rendered, and the useEffect is called again. That being said, in the preceding example, you could call a function when the new component state is rendered using useEffectcleanup function. Let's take a look at an example to understand it in a better way:

```
const App: React.FC = props => {

const [counter, setCounter] = useState(0)

  useEffect(() => {

    document.title = 'Counter is at ' + counter

    return function cleanup() {

      console.log(`This will fire whenever this function gets called next/the component unmounts. Counter is ${counter} right now`)

    }

  }, [counter])

  return <>

<span>{ counter }</span>
```

```
<button onClick={() =>setCounter(c => c + 1)}>Increment Counter</button>
</>
}
```

When running this code initially, we would see nothing in the console, like the following:

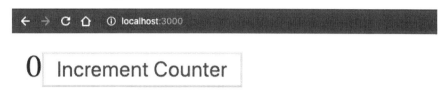

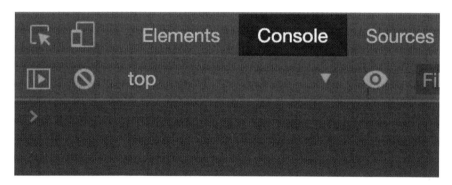

Figure 3.6

But once I click on the **Increment** counter, something interesting would show up in the console:

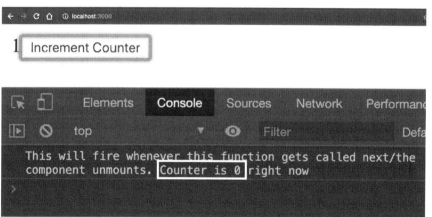

Figure 3.7

Alright! We see that on the screen, the counter is actually 1. But in the console, we receive the log with the counter value of 0. Did we miss something? Is this a bug? Actually no, this is expected behaviour.

Well, you could see that the purpose of the cleanup function is to remove anything you want to get rid of before the *new instance* of that thing is created. Hence, React needs to call the cleanup function of the older useEffect function so that it could access the old subscription variable and that environment. React obviously should not fire the cleanup function of the latest useEffect function because well, it does not require a cleanup yet, does it?

useCallback

Remember how we passed a dependency array in useEffect hook to let React know about the variables we cared about? This let React not to run the effect functions again and again when they were not required. But what about the functions you call inside the useEffect function itself? It is easy to miss things like these:

```
const [result, setResult] = useState(null)

const [url, setUrl] = useState(null)

  async function someAsyncOperation() {

    // some more code

    return await fetch(url)

  }

  useEffect(() => {

    // some long code....

someAsyncOperation().then(r => {

setResult(r)

    })

  }, [])
```

Oops! Can you point out the problem in the code snippet that might occur? You see, although looking at the effect function it seems like no dependency is required (well, because we're not using any state variable directly, upon closely looking we could see that we're actually using the state variable urlinside the someAsyncOpeartion function! That means, if somewhere setResult was called, the effect function would not re-run hence not re-fetch the URL and hence would produce a buggy output.

This could happen and is usually hard to notice as your codebase grows. So how to ensure that you don't miss adding the dependency in the useEffect hook? You don't. You pass the function as a dependency because it makes more sense that way! You see, the behaviour of the actual function someAsyncOperation changes due to the change in the state url variable, and hence it should be the one which should be added as a dependency. Not only this simplifies things but seems more logical.

However, there's no way React could compare a function with the previous version without actually executing it and seeing the result, but once you execute the function anyway, there's no point in going back. Remember how we solved this similar issue in useEffect? Yes, dependencies array to the rescue! But how do we specify a dependency array for a standalone function?

Here, you could use a new hook called useCallback. This hook would allow you to create memorized functions which would only change its identity if the dependency array passed to it changes. Here's the same example from above but this time with a memorized function:

```
constsomeAsyncOperation = useCallback(async () => {
    // some more code
    return await fetch(url)
}, [url])
useEffect(() => {
    // some long code....
someAsyncOperation().then(r => {
setResult(r)
})
}, [someAsyncOperation])
```

Here, we could see that we're now passing someAsyncOperation as the dependency of the main side effect function, and we're passing url as the dependency of the someAsyncOperation function itself. This keeps things in order and allows you to write readable and clean code.

React has a bunch of more inbuilt hooks which we'll take a look at eventually as we proceed in the coming chapters.

Custom hooks

Now that we have a working knowledge of React hooks and how they work under the hood, it is fairly simple to create simple custom hooks for your own use case. Let's start with a simple example. Remember we talked about how useState doesn't provide a callback function when the state is updated? Let's implement that as a custom hook.

```
import { useState, useEffect } from 'react'

constuseStateCB = (initState: any, cb: Function) => {

const [state, setState] = useState(initState)

useEffect(() =>cb(state), [state])

  return [state, setState]

}

export default useStateCB
```

We could create something like the above in a file called useStateCB.ts and import this *hook* anywhere and use it! So how does it work?

When you call useStateCB("test", updatedState =>console. log(updateState)), what you're doing is you're setting up twohooks - the original useState hook and the useEffect hook. The useEffect hook is used to keep a *watch* over our useState hook, and once the *state* changes we call the pass callback function with the new state. Because remember? The useEffect hook always runs withthe latest state value once per render. In this way, you can tailor custom hooks to your needs using some basic fundamental hooks.

Class components

Here's a quick example of a class based component written in TypeScript + React:

```
import React from 'react'

import ReactDOM from 'react-dom'

class App extends React.Component<{}, {}> {
```

```
  render() {

    return <p>Hello World</p>

  }

}

ReactDOM.render(<App />, document.getElementById('root'))
```

Here, we create a component named App which extends the class React.Component. Upon looking, you'd find that React.Component class provides a lot of useful features which enables us to use lifecycle methods and state inside class based components. We could specify the types of our props and types of our state here <{}, {}>.

Props

We discussed in functional components about props and how they're simply a small piece of data that a component could pass on to its children and how it could define itself as well. Here's another example which receives a prop:

```
class App extends React.Component<{ prop1: string }, {}> {

  render() {

    return <p>Hello World. Prop1 says {this.props.prop1}</p>

  }

}

ReactDOM.render(<App prop1="something" />, document.
getElementById('root'))
```

We specified the types of props which we could receive using TypeScript and then we passed prop1 when rendering the component. Finally, we accessed the passed prop using this.props object. The this. props object is populated by React with the keys being the names of props and values being the value passed with them.

Just like in the functional way, you could pass anything, even functions, as props as JavaScript has first class functions.

Additionally, we see that we have a method called render which is responsible for what the UI is displayed by React. No matter what you do in a class based component, whatever you return from the render method is the only thing which would be visible to the user on the screen (unless obviously you try to modify the DOM directly by yourself - which is of course a bad practice when using React)

State

Managing state in class components is very straightforward. Out of the box, React allows you to create a specially named variable called state. React also provides a setState function which allows the mutation of the state object by React (and subsequent re-render). If you're wondering from where this implementation comes, you could see that we inherit from the React.Component class, which contains the functionality mentioned.

Here's a simple example demonstrating the state in a class based component:

```
class App extends React.Component<{}, { name: string }> {
    state = {
        name: 'Mehul'
    }
    render() {
        return <p>{this.state.name}</p>
    }
}
```

Here we could see once again that we could specify the type of the state in TypeScript, and then we could go ahead and initialize our state with the defaults. So where's the difference? The difference comes when we start using this.setState function. Upon calling that, React will update our state object and would automatically re-render and apply the updates to the component if necessary. For example:

```
class App extends React.Component<{}, { num: number }> {
    state = {
num: Math.random()
    }
changeNum() {
    this.setState({
```

```
num: Math.random()
    })
  }
  render() {
    return <p onClick={() =>this.changeNum()}>{this.state.num}</p>
  }
}
```

On clicking the p tag, we'll see that the state variable changes the num property and sets it to a new Math.random value. See how it is different from a functional component. In a functional component, the state is never mutated, instead in a new render, the hooks return different (and updated) values. In class based components however, React itself mutates the this keyword to update the props and state according to the correct behaviour. This shows that although functional and class based components might just look like syntactic sugar over one another, fundamentally they're very different from each other at their core of working.

Lifecycle methods

React provides a bunch of lifecycle methods for you to put your code in and take full control over the rendering mechanism of the components. Let's start with those and see a quick example in every component. Additionally, we could explore how they differ from hooks and what could be a possible behaviour replacement for hooks.

constructor

If you're coming from an OOP background, you'll know constructor is the first method which runs whenever you create an object. Although JavaScript doesn't follow class-based inheritance, the syntactic sugar it introduced with classes in ES6 resembles pretty closely to the same pattern.

This is not a lifecycle method provided by React, but rather the language itself. However, you could do all of the initialization work here, that is, initializing your state, setting up any global event listeners (like window resize, and so on) and get ready for your component to get mounted.

static getDerivedStateFromProps

This method was added in v16.3 and simply allows you to update the state to match the props if required. The method getDerivedStateFromProps runs before the render method both on the first mount and subsequent mounts. It is static and you should not perform side effects (like animations or network requests) in this method.

Infact, React docs recommend that in mostcases you don't need to implement this lifecycle method anyway. Most of your work could be done by the other ones we'll discuss now:

```
static getDerivedStateFromProps(props, state) {

  if (props.email !== state.email) {

   return {

    email: props.email

   }

  }

  return null

}
```

You see that we return null if there's no update, indicating that we do not intend to update the state of the component. Whatever you return would be updated as the state of the component.

render

This is the only method which is mandatory to be present in a class based React component. That is because React is a UI library and the point of using a component is to spit out some visual information to the user. So if you're using React component, render method is a must to define. Whatever you return from this method gets displayed on the screen. Here's a simple example:

```
render() {

    return <p>Hello world!</p>

}
```

getSnapshotBeforeUpdate

React calls this method before react actually writes anything to the browser, that is, to the DOM. At this point, render has been called but the DOM has not been updated. Again, as the docs says, this method as specific use cases only, but it's always good to know about the available methods. You have to return a "snapshot" value from this method which then you'll be able to access in another lifecycle method called componentDidUpdate. Here's an example:

```
getSnapshotBeforeUpdate(prevProps, prevState) {

  if (prevProps.prop1 !== this.props.prop1) {

    return "Prop mismatch";

  }

  return null

}
```

Returning null indicates that there was no snapshot to be captured. And then we could access it in the componentDidUpdate as we'll see now.

componentDidMount

The method componentDidMount is called once react is finished mounting the component. But not so fast! The component is still not visible to the user as it has not been written to the DOM yet. So what does it mean to be mounted? It means that the component has been mounted in the virtual DOM of the React and is ready to be pushed to the DOM. At this moment, if you call setState, React would perform a component re-render but would not show the intermediate state of the component.

componentDidUpdate

This method is called by React when your component updates. On the initial mount, this method is not called. This gets called with three parameters - prevProps, prevState and snapshot which are previous props, previous component state and the snapshot from getSnapshotBeforeUpdate method as discussed above. Here's a simple example:

```
componentDidUpdate(prevProps, prevState, snapshot) {
```

```
if (this.props.id !== prevProps.id) {

  // perform a new network request and update state

  }

}
```

componentWillUnmount

As the name suggests, this method is fired when your component is being unmounted. This is the best place for cleanup of global event listeners, cancelling network requests and timers, and so on. This is the last lifecycle React would ever call in a component's lifetime.

Here's a beautiful open source illustration I found for lifecycle methods of React:

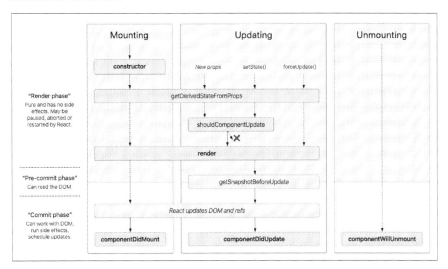

Figure 3.8

Conclusion

This chapter was an important one as it introduced us to components - functional and class based. Additionally, we learned about hooks, how they work under the hood and how you could create custom hooks. Further, we saw how to work with class based components as well and why React sees functional components as the future of the library. We'll keep covering more React topics in depth in the chapters further.

Questions

1. What is the difference between class and functional components?

2. Transpile the following into valid JS: <p><span>Hello</span> World</p>

3. Is useState synchronous? Why/Why not?

4. What does the dependencies array of useEffect hook do?

Does the useEffect hook run before or after the component is rendered/updated?

Why does hook have no "lifecycle methods" concept? How does it differ fundamentally from the class-based model of lifecycles?

CHAPTER 4

Application State Management in React

In the last chapter, we got our basic and solid understanding of components and the ways to create and work with them. One thing we noticed is that most components are truly useful when they have some sort of state associated with them, that is, the components "remember". That being said, React does a great job with the hooks like useState and the this.state object for functional and class-based components, respectively. But as your code grows, there's a necessity of managing state in a more organized way, avoid prop drilling and make things cleaner, especially when there has to be an information exchange among different components at different levels of nesting.

This could be referred to as managing the state of the application. Let's see how we could work with it.

Structure

- Communication between components
- Using Context API
  - createContext
  - useContext

- useReducer hook
- Redux as an alternative

Objectives

In this chapter, we aim to cover basic out of the box functionality which react provides us to manage state in our applications. In most of the cases, it would be all one would need for his/her projects, and even a bit beyond. For very advanced cases, we'll use a reducer based pattern like Redux. Since React 16.8 hooks, React provides an out of the box solution similar (but less powerful) to redux. Let's learn all about that in this chapter.

Communication between components

If you think about it, managing application state is roughly another way of saying effective communication of some information among a lot of components.

Although you could have a local state in components, things get tricky when you want to communicate between components, especially when it is up the component hierarchy or even be very far relatives in the tree. This happens all the time. Consider you logout from a website using a link in the content area, this information should be dispatched to the header, which is a completely different component, so that header could update the links back to the ones to be shown to an unauthenticated user.

Let's see some common ways we'll learn in this chapter to communicate between the components:

- Props (parent to child data flow)
- Refs (Calling child methods from a parent)
- Context API
- Redux (Centralized state) (in later chapters)

It is interesting to note that with a slight trick, it is possible to use Context API to have two-way communication, however redux is truly decoupled and centralized state store. Redux is the go-to choice for intermediate to advanced applications because of its unidirectional data flow (careful! This doesn't mean that it can only communicate in one way), centralized state share and great debugging tools. Let's take a look at props first.

Prop drilling

Imagine you have a UI theme in your React application which holds values like colours and font sizes. Now, of course, these values need to be accessed by respective input fields and textareas. However, getting to those input fields in the first place in the hierarchy of the elements is a cumbersome task. You'll need to drill your fontSize prop all the way down to the input field, even though none of the components in between needs to be aware ofit. Let's see what this is.

It is the most naivetechnique in sharing data among components. You use props to pass down data to the child components. Consider this very simple example:

```
import React from 'react'

import ReactDOM from 'react-dom'

const App: React.FC<{ name: string, age: number }> = props => {

  return <div>

<p>We've got all of your information!</p>

<Profile name={props.name} age={props.age} />

</div>

}

const Profile: React.FC<{ name: string, age: number }> = props => {

  return <div>

<p>Here's a complete information about you</p>

<p>We save everything in our databases</p>

<NameFormatter name={props.name} />

<AgeFormatter age={props.age} />

</div>

}

constNameFormatter: React.FC<{ name: string }> = props => {

  return <p>Like you can see, here's your name: <TextField value={props.name}
```

```
type="text" /></p>

}

constAgeFormatter: React.FC<{ age: number }> = props => {

  return <p>Your age is: <TextField value={props.age} type="number" /></p>

}

constTextField: React.FC<{ value: any, type: string }> = props => {

  return <input type={props.type} value={props.value} />

}

ReactDOM.render(<App name="Mehul" age={20} />, document.
getElementById('root'))
```

If you observe here, you'd realize that the component App and Profile never needed to know about the props name and age. It was only NameFormatter and AgeFormatter, which required the respective values to render the UI correctly. However, because the props name and age are available at the App component level, in order to reach to NameFormatter and AgeFormatter component levels, you need to *drill* it down to them.

This practice refers to prop drilling and usually is not required with the more advanced and sophisticated methods we have now for communication between components at the different hierarchical level. Let's take a look at the different methods which could help us prevent situations like these.

Refs

Ref in react refers to creating a reference to something. A ref is an escape hatch from React, allowing you to peek directly inside the component or DOM, whatever you like. Hence, it should be handled with care. Because the things you do with refs areusually following imperative patterns, it kind of breaks the way react wants you to work with it - declaratively. But sometimes, it is very useful to go out the way a little because there's only so much React could bring to the table cooked within itself.

Using refs, not only could we communicate with the DOM directly, but we could also allow a parent to call a child's method. We know that we could do it easily the other way using props, but it cannot be done using props for child component method which needs to be called by a parent. Let's take a look at this example:

This is Parent.tsx file:

```tsx
// Parent.tsx
import React, { useRef } from 'react'
import ReactDOM from 'react-dom'
import ChildInput, { ChildInputHandles } from './Child'
const Parent: React.FC = () => {
const ref = useRef<ChildInputHandles>(null)
 function setChildFocus() {
   if (ref.current) {
ref.current.setFocus()
   }
 }
  return <div>
<ChildInput ref={ref} defaultValue="Hello World" />
<button onClick={setChildFocus}>Set focus to input</button>
</div>
}
ReactDOM.render(<Parent />, document.getElementById('root'))
```

And the Child.tsx file:

```tsx
// Child.tsx
import React, { RefForwardingComponent, forwardRef, useImperativeHandle, useRef } from 'react'
export interface ChildInputHandles {
setFocus(): void
}
export interface ChildInputProps {
defaultValue: string
}
constChildInput: RefForwardingComponent<ChildInputHandles, ChildInputProps> = (props, ref) => {
```

```
constinputRef = useRef<HTMLInputElement>(null)

useImperativeHandle(ref, () => ({

setFocus() {

        if (inputRef.current) {

inputRef.current.focus()

    }

  }

 }))

    return <input {...props} defaultValue={props.defaultValue} ref={inputRef} />

}

export default forwardRef(ChildInput)
```

Let's take a look what's happening here:

1. In Parent.tsx file, we first import the ChildRef component and give it a ref using the useRef hook. We use <ChildInputHandles> to type the methods and props we could access via ourref. current variable.

2. We have a method setChildFocus function in Parent which actually uses refs to penetrate into the child component and call the specified function, that is,setFocus inside the child.

3. In the ChildInput component, we type it as RefForwardingComponent as the TypeScript type to type the receiving props and props available via ref forwarding.

4. We use another hook called useImperativeHandle which accepts our passed ref (see the second argument of ChildInput component) and binds certain methods which we could directly call on that ref inside the parent.

5. Finally, we use a regular inputRef ref inside the Child itself to actually enable the focus inside the definition of setFocus inside the Child component.

In this way, we could use the refs as an escape hatch to access functions and values inside children from parent components. However, approaches like these are usually not recommended in most scenarios and really put forward the thought that there's a better way to implement whatever the developer is trying to do.

Let us now move on to Context API and see how to use it to create *worm-holes* in data passing.

Context API

In prop drilling example, we saw how a UI theme would need to drill its props all the way down to a component which actually needs it, exposing it to all other components which don't even need to know about those values. Meet Context in React. Context allows you to create wormholes of data in components, that is, you could teleport data from one component to another down the tree without the intermediate components knowing about the transferred data.

Let's see the code first and understand how context API works in general by taking a look at this mini-application:

This is our index.tsx file:

```
import React from 'react'

import ReactDOM from 'react-dom'

import Component1 from './Component1'

ReactDOM.render(<Component1 />, document.getElementById('root'))
```

This is our Component1.tsx file:

```
import React from 'react'

import Header from './Header'

import Content from './Content'

import Footer from './Footer'

import './global.css'

constComponent1: React.FC = () => {

   return (

<div>

<Header />

<Content />

<Footer />

</div>

   )
```

```
}
```

export default Component1

This is our Header.tsx file:

```
import React from 'react'
const Header: React.FC = () => {
   return (
<header>
<h1>Welcome to my site!</h1>
<p>Hello mehul</p>
</header>
   )
}
```

export default Header

This is our Content.tsx file:

```
import React from 'react'
import Sidebar from './Sidebar'
import RightArticle from './RightArticle'
const Content: React.FC = () => {
   return (
<section>
<Sidebar />
<RightArticle />
</section>
   )
}
```

export default Content

This is our Sidebar.tsx file:

```
import React from 'react'
const Sidebar: React.FC = () => {
   return (
```

```
<aside>
<h2>Wow this is a nice sidebar</h2>
<p>See my logo</p>
<imgsrc="https://codedamn.com/assets/images/red-logo.png" />
</aside>
    )
}
export default Sidebar
```

This is our RightArticle.tsx file:

```
import React from 'react'
constRightArticle: React.FC = () => {
    return (
<article>
<h2>This is my site!</h2>
<p>It is very nice</p>
<p>The mode right now is: light</p>
<button>Click here to turn on dark mode</button>
</article>
    )
}
export default RightArticle
```

This is our Footer.tsx file:

```
import React from 'react'
const Footer: React.FC = () => {
    return (
<footer>
<p>Copyright &copy; Me.</p>
<imgsrc="https://codedamn.com/assets/images/red-logo.png" />
</footer>
    )
```

```
}
```

export default Footer

And finally, to add some CSS, this is our stylesheet global.css:

```css
* {
    margin: 0;
    padding: 0;
    font-family: Arial;
}
header {
    text-align: center;
    padding: 10px;
    border-bottom: 1px solid #eee;
}
section {
    min-height: 80vh;
    display: flex;
    width: 960px;
    margin: 10px auto;
    justify-content: space-between;
}
article {
    flex-grow: 1;
    margin-left: 10px;
    background: rgb(226, 226, 226);
}
aside {
    max-width: 250px;
    background: rgb(226, 226, 226);
}
img {
```

```
  height: 80px;
}
footer {
  display: flex;
  flex-direction: row-reverse;
  justify-content: center;
  align-items: center;
}
footer img {
  height: 50px;
  margin-right: 20px;
}
```

This would roughly render something like this on your screens:

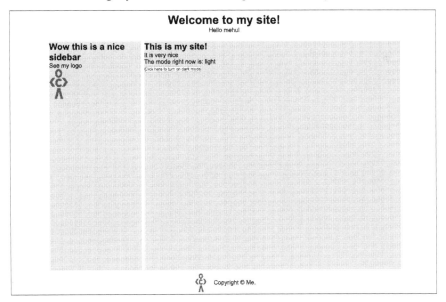

Figure 4.1

And for your clarity, here's how the file structure looks:

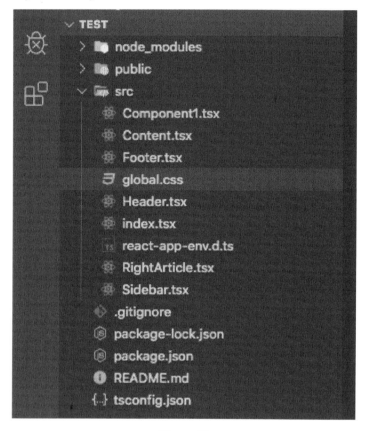

Figure 4.2

Notice that we're using create-react-app.

Okay, so now you can see we have a button saying **Click here to turn on dark mode**. On clicking this, we would add **dark** class to our body and the CSS would take care from there. But what about other changes? Like we want to change the logo from red logo to white logo if we're indark mode, give the Header component the logged in (assumed) user's username, and make sure the article component knows about the global dark mode state.

Let's use context API to fill these gaps. We'll create a context which we would be usedin different components.

Context.Provider

Building upon our previous work, let's take a look at our Component1. tsx file:

```
import React, { createContext, useState } from 'react'

import Header from './Header'

import Content from './Content'

import Footer from './Footer'

import './global.css'

type Context = {

  theme: string

  name: string

  logo: string

}

constStateContext = createContext<Partial<Context>>({})

export { StateContext }

constComponent1: React.FC = () => {

const [theme, setTheme] = useState<string>('light')

const defaults = {

    get theme() {

      return theme

    },

    set theme(value) {

document.body.classList.remove('dark', 'light')

document.body.classList.add(value)

setTheme(value)

    },

    name: 'Mehul',

    get logo() {

      return this.theme === 'dark' ? 'white-logo' : 'red-logo'

    }
```

```
  }
  return (
<StateContext.Provider value={defaults}>
<Header />
<Content />
<Footer />
</StateContext.Provider>
  )
}
```

export default Component1

You see, we've added another variable named context outside the component definition, which has the value of createContext({}).

This creates a consumer and provider which you could use across the app to access the data. Let's see how.

We supply a type to this using TypeScript that indicates the value we'll be using inside this context. This would also be used as the default value for this context; we don't specify it in the Provider.

When we call createContext, it creates two React elements, Context. Provider and Context.Consumer. Whenever you wrap elements inside Context.Provider, you can access that particular context inside the child elements. As you can see above, we wrapped our app essentially in <StateContext.Provider>.

With the useContext hook, however, we can access the consumer part of the context in a breeze. See the following usage of useContext.

useContexthook

Our updated Header.tsx file:

import React, { useContext } from 'react'

import { StateContext } from './Component1'

const Header: React.FC = () => {

const state = useContext(StateContext)

  return (

```
<header>
<h1>Welcome to my site!</h1>
<p>Hello {state.name}</p>
</header>
  )
}
```

export default Header

See how convenient it is to access the name! It gets really interesting once we add dynamic functionality to play. Let's modify our CSS file first for dark mode:

```
/* existing css here */
/* dark mode */
.dark {
   background: black;
color: rgb(194, 194, 194);
}
.dark header {
   border-bottom: 1px solid rgb(56, 56, 56);
}
.dark aside, .dark article {
   background: rgb(53, 53, 53);
}
```

And now, let's make the button functional on RightArticle.tsx:

```
import React, { useContext } from 'react'
import { StateContext } from './Component1'
constRightArticle: React.FC = () => {
const state = useContext(StateContext)
   function toggleTheme() {
      if(state.theme === 'dark') {
state.theme = 'light'
      } else {
```

```
state.theme = 'dark'
    }
  }
  return (
<article>
<h2>This is my site!</h2>
<p>It is very nice</p>
<p>The mode right now is: {state.theme}</p>
<button onClick={toggleTheme}>Click here to turn on dark mode</button>
</article>
  )
}
export default RightArticle
```

Finally, we could implement the image part as well:

Sidebar.tsx

```
import React, { useContext } from 'react'
import { StateContext } from './Component1'
const Sidebar: React.FC = () => {
const { logo } = useContext(StateContext)
  return (
<aside>
<h2>Wow this is a nice sidebar</h2>
<p>See my logo</p>
<imgsrc={`https://codedamn.com/assets/images/${logo}.png`} />
</aside>
  )
}
export default Sidebar
```

And Footer.tsx:

```
import React, { useContext } from 'react'
import { StateContext } from './Component1'
```

```
const Footer: React.FC = () => {

const { logo } = useContext(StateContext)

  return (

<footer>

<p>Copyright &copy; Me.</p>

<imgsrc={`https://codedamn.com/assets/images/${logo}.png`} />

</footer>

  )

}

export default Footer
```

That's it! You could see how easy it is for parents to pass values to children and how easy it is for children to modify values which would then allow parents to behave accordingly. This is how the site looks in both dark and light mode:

Light mode

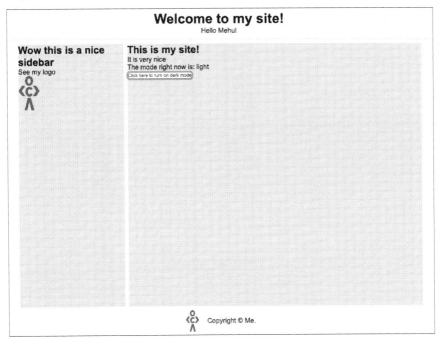

Figure 4.3: Light mode

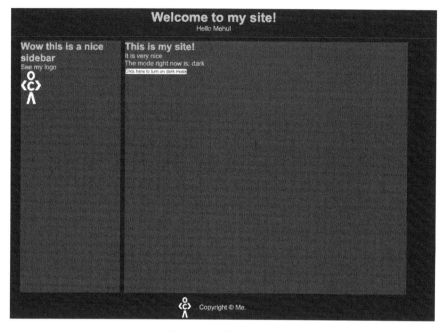

Figure 4.4: Dark mode

useReducer hook

Now that we've seen how useContext works, we can streamline our state of the application even further by using yet another inbuilt hook called useReducer provided by React.

Let's start by decoupling our createContext from the above example into a different file:

This is our state.ts file:

```
import { createContext } from 'react'

type Context = {

  theme: string

  name: string

  logo: string

}

constinitialState = {

  theme: 'light',
```

```
    name: 'Mehul',

    logo: 'red-logo'

}

function stateFunc(state: Context, action: { type: string, payload: any }) {

const { type, payload } = action

    switch(type) {

        case 'SET_THEME':

document.body.classList.remove('dark', 'light')

document.body.classList.add(payload)

            return {

                ...state,

                theme: payload,

                logo: payload === 'dark' ? 'white-logo' : 'red-logo'

            }

    }

    return initialState

}

constStateContext = createContext<{ state: Context, dispatch: Function}>({

    state: initialState,

    dispatch: () => 0

})

export const Provider = StateContext.Provider

export const reducer = stateFunc

export const context = StateContext

export constdefaultState = initialState
```

A lot of stuff is going on in this file! Let's see what's happening here:

1. First of all, there's a regular function called stateFunc which takes a state as the input and action as the input.

2. The action object consists of **type** as string and **payload** as any value. (You could narrow this down even more by specifying stricter types for type and payloads).

3. Now, on the basis of the type, we have certain cases, if the type is SET_THEME, we do update the state and return it. This becomes our updated state. How? That is done by the useReducer hook which we'll see in a minute.

4. Finally, we have our old StateContext, but this time, instead of holding just the state, our context holds two values. The state and a dispatch function.

5. The state is our original state object, and dispatch is a method which is used to update the state. You see, here, we don't interact with the state directly, instead, we send certain "actions" which in turn update the state.

We initialize the dispatch method with a garbage function, but we'll overwrite that eventually when we're using the context provider, so it doesn't matter.

Now, coming back to Component1.tsx file, this is how it would look like:

```
import React, { useReducer } from 'react'

import Header from './Header'

import Content from './Content'

import Footer from './Footer'

import './global.css'

import { Provider, defaultState, reducer } from './state'

constComponent1: React.FC = () => {

const [state, dispatch] = useReducer(reducer, defaultState)

   return (

<Provider value={{ state, dispatch }}>

<Header />

<Content />

<Footer />

</Provider>

   )

}

export default Component1
```

Now you can see we're making use of a new hook called useReducer. What this hook does is, it returns us an array with two elements in it, just like we had for useState hook. The first element is the state, and the second element is the dispatch function.

One major difference here between useState and useReducer is that with useState, your second function is the setter of your state, that is, whatever you pass as the argument in the function in case of useState gets set as the state, whereas in useReducer, whenever you call dispatch method, useReducer calls your reducer on it, and then whatever you return from the reducer method gets set as the state. Consider this:

```
const [state, setState] = useState(0)

setState(1) // ← sets the state variable to 1

const [state, dispatch] = useReducer(reducer, 1)

dispatch({ type: 'do something', value: 100 }) // Now reducer is called

// behind the scenes: reducer(state, { type: 'do something', value: 100 }) ->
returns 101

// state becomes 101
```

This is important for large data management, as now you could have much finer control over your data flow.

Let's now update other files to work accordingly with the useReducer hook:

Footer.tsx:

```
import React, { useContext } from 'react'

import { context } from './state'

const Footer: React.FC = () => {

const { state: { logo } } = useContext(context)

    return (

<footer>

<p>Copyright &copy; Me.</p>

<imgsrc={`https://codedamn.com/assets/images/${logo}.png`} />

</footer>

    )

}
```

```
export default Footer
```

Header.tsx:

```
import React, { useContext } from 'react'
import { context } from './state'
const Header: React.FC = () => {
const { state: { name } } = useContext(context)
   return (
<header>
<h1>Welcome to my site!</h1>
<p>Hello {name}</p>
</header>
   )
}
export default Header
```

RightArticle.tsx:

```
import React, { useContext } from 'react'
import { context } from './state'
constRightArticle: React.FC = () => {
const { state: { theme }, dispatch } = useContext(context)
   function toggleTheme() {
     if(theme === 'dark') {
        dispatch({ type: 'SET_THEME', payload: 'light' })
     } else {
        dispatch({ type: 'SET_THEME', payload: 'dark' })
     }
   }
   return (
<article>
<h2>This is my site!</h2>
<p>It is very nice</p>
<p>The mode right now is: {theme}</p>
```

```
<button onClick={toggleTheme}>Click here to turn on dark mode</button>
</article>
  )
}
export default RightArticle
```

See how we're making use of the dispatch function above? That calls our reducer on it, and our reducer modifies the state which is propagated to the components using it!

And Sidebar.tsx:

```
import React, { useContext } from 'react'
import { context } from './state'
const Sidebar: React.FC = () => {
const { state: { logo } } = useContext(context)
  return (
<aside>
<h2>Wow this is a nice sidebar</h2>
<p>See my logo</p>
<imgsrc={`https://codedamn.com/assets/images/${logo}.png`} />
</aside>
  )
}
export default Sidebar
```

Once we complete all these changes, we'll see that we still have the same output on the screen. But consider this. It's now so easy to implement even more stateful things in the application. For example, let's say you want to change the logged in name on clicking of a button.

You'll simply get to the dispatch method in any component and dispatch an action with a type, say, CHANGE_USERNAME and a payload of whatever you wish to do.

Now in a completely different file, that is, state.tsx you'll add to your reducer what you wish to do when action is CHANGE_USERNAME as follows:

```
switch(type) {
// ..
  case 'CHANGE_USERNAME':
   return {
    ...state,
    name: payload
   }
// ....
}
```

And you're done! It couldn't get more streamlined than this!

Conclusion

In this chapter, we learned about how we could leverage inbuilt React solutions like Context API to implement very streamlined state management without any external libraries. In the further chapters, we'll be looking at how to use more sophisticated technologies with React to achieve even more.

Questions

1. What is Context API from React?

2. How does useReducer hook work?

3. What is Context.Consumer? How does Context.Provider differs from Context.Consumer?

CHAPTER 5

Server Side React

So far we've seen how React works on the frontend, various ways to work with React, managing state with it and even created a little working front page for us! There's so much more we could do we react, especially once we move it to the server-side. Now it is strange to think about React on the server, at least it was for me when I was first introduced to the concept! What does it even mean to use React on a server? And what benefits does it provide us? We'll answer everything on this and more in this chapter. Let's get started.

In this chapter we'll explore how we can move React to a server, essentially using Node.js to render React code before we send it to the browsers so that we give users and search engine crawlers a seamless experience in seeing our content immediately.

Structure

- Server-side rendering
- Why it is required
- Hello world with SSR
- How ReactDOMServer works
- Adding more components to SSR
- Routing
- Hydrating ReactDOM
- Fetching data

Objective

This chapter aims to introduce you to the concept of server-side rendering using React and discuss why it is a good option to go about if you're just starting off with a project and need SEO and performance to be of no-compromise-area. We'll see how we can do Hello World with React SSR by creating a very simple project, and then proceed to add more and more functionality to it. Finally, we would conclude with the strong argument why it is a good idea to choose a server-side rendering framework like Next.js for React to work on medium to large scale SSR apps built with React.

React on Server

Currently, what happens when you use a react application is the following:

1. You visit the page (let's say http://example.com)

2. The page makes a request to the remote server.

3. The remote server sends you just a little HTML response like this:

```
<!doctype html><html lang="en"><head><meta charset="utf-8"/><link rel="shortcut icon"
href="/favicon.ico"/><meta name="viewport" content="width=device-width,initial-scale=1"/><meta
name="theme-color" content="#000000"/><link rel="manifest" href="/manifest.json"/><title>React
App</title><link href="/static/css/main.ac96f7b6.chunk.css" rel="stylesheet"/></head><body>
<noscript>You need to enable JavaScript to run this app.</noscript><div id="root"></div>
<script>!function(l){function e(e){for(var r,t,n=e[0],o=e[1],u=e[2],f=0,i=
[];f<n.length;f++)t=n[f],p[t]&&i.push(p[t][0]),p[t]=0;for(r in
o)Object.prototype.hasOwnProperty.call(o,r)&&(l[r]=o[r]);for(s&&s(e);i.length;)i.shift()();return
c.push.apply(c,u||[]),a()}function a(){for(var e,r=0;r<c.length;r++){for(var
t=c[r],n=!0,o=1;o<t.length;o++){var u=t[o];0!==p[u]&&(n=!1)}n&&(c.splice(r--,1),e=f(f.s=t[0]))}return
e}var t={},p={1:0},c=[];function f(e){if(t[e])return t[e].exports;var r=t[e]={i:e,l:!1,exports:
{}};return l[e].call(r.exports,r,r.exports,f),r.l=!0,r.exports}f.m=l,f.c=t,f.d=function(e,r,t)
{f.o(e,r)||Object.defineProperty(e,r,{enumerable:!0,get:t})},f.r=function(e){"undefined"!=typeof
Symbol&&Symbol.toStringTag&&Object.defineProperty(e,Symbol.toStringTag,
{value:"Module"}),Object.defineProperty(e,"__esModule",{value:!0})},f.t=function(r,e){if(1&e&&
(r=f(r)),8&e)return r;if(4&e&&"object"==typeof r&&r&&r.__esModule)return r;var
t=Object.create(null);if(f.r(t),Object.defineProperty(t,"default",
{enumerable:!0,value:r}),2&e&&"string"!=typeof r)for(var n in r)f.d(t,n,function(e){return
r[e]}.bind(null,n));return t},f.n=function(e){var r=e&&e.__esModule?function(){return
e.default}:function(){return e};return f.d(r,"a",r),r},f.o=function(e,r){return
Object.prototype.hasOwnProperty.call(e,r)},f.p="/";var r=window.webpackJsonp=window.webpackJsonp||
[],n=r.push.bind(r);r.push=e,r=r.slice();for(var o=0;o<r.length;o++)e(r[o]);var s=n;a()}([])</script>
<script src="/static/js/2.b41502e9.chunk.js"></script><script
src="/static/js/main.28647029.chunk.js"></script></body></html>
```

Figure 5.1

4. Your browser understands this request, and if you look closely, you'll see that the request contains no readable content whatsoever. It is just linking to a bunch of CSS and JS files only.

5. Your browser downloads those JS files.

6. Your browser parses and runs those JS files (which is actually React code you wrote)

7. Depending on the React code, your browser makes another HTTP request to the server to bring in the data required by the React app.

8. Finally, when the data is available, first meaningful content render is done to the user.

9. The DOM is now populated with all the HTML you expect to see. Here's an example from codedamn.com which uses React:

The actual response from the server:

Figure 5.2

The rendered DOM finally:

Figure 5.3

This approach is definitely fine. But there exists an alternate way to do things. The reason you chose react is because of its flexibility and robustness, which lies under the hood. But what if you want a completely rendered page instead of letting the browser go to and fro for every request?

Here, **Server Side Rendering** (**SSR**) comes into place. As the name suggests, Server Side Rendering basically means your server renders your React code into the DOM-like code you saw above, so that browser could directly render it without any/minimal JS support. Before that, let's answer some common SSR questions.

What is Server-Side Rendering?

As the name says, you are rendering the page on the server and delivering it to the client, instead of letting the client (browser) render the page itself using JavaScript you wrote. Server-Side Rendering takes one step from the client back into the server, that is, parsing the React code logic. In its very essence, SSR means the backend is doing most of the job and delivering the pages to the frontend, instead of the client making heavy use of JS for routing and state management. That was how applications using PHP used to work back in the days. But with enhancement in JS standards and better-performing devices and smartphones, client-side rendering is becoming much more popular these days.

Why Server Side Rendering?

If client-side rendering is so good, why are we considering server-side rendering in the 2020 decade? Well, SSR has its own benefits which cannot be ignored, some of them includes:

1. SEO: Search engines love reading HTML markup and making sense of the page out of that. Most of the search engines, except advanced ones like Google, cannot really interpret a lot of JavaScript and hence have to rely heavily on what your "source code" says. And since for client-side websites, source code doesn't say anything at all, the search engines are not able to index your site which impacts your rankings.

2. Performance: There is an obvious boost in performance when you're using SSR. Since SSR involves rendering a page already before delivering, you don't have to worry about different browser support, different device support APIs, etc. in your JS code, because most of them never get delivered anyway.

Hence, for compatibility reasons with search engines, it is most important to have SSR implemented, so that you can get the best of both worlds.

Starting with SSR

SSR with React is tricky without any framework. But still, we would begin with that just so that we know what happens under the hood when we're working with other frameworks. Before starting off, we'll focus on one special thing in React, ReactDOM.

ReactDOM

When we do ReactDOM.render(<App />, element), we're effectively telling React to match the DOM tree (what you see as UI of the web app) with the host tree (what is contained in JavaScript as your React code)

We discussed above how App unfolds into a nested object (a tree, essentially). ReactDOM is one of the renderers of that particular tree. Can you think of any other example? React Native could be thought of as another complete renderer.

There's another renderer called ReactDOMServer. ReactDOMServer, as the name says, enables you to write React code and then, instead of rendering it into a browser like an environment, render it as a string on a server to be sent to the client as (close to) static markup.

Let us now configure our very first server-side rendering React app.

SSR project configuration

1. Go ahead and create an empty directory named react-ssr

2. Using your terminal, cd into that

3. Do a npminit -y to initialize it with default npm configuration

Let's install the relevant npm packages first, run the following command:

npm install react react-dom express --save

And the other dev dependencies would include:

npm install @babel/core @babel/preset-react @babel/register webpack webpack-cli --save-dev

At this point, your package.json dependency and devDependency section should look roughly like this:

```
"dependencies": {

    "express": "^4.16.3",

    "react": "^16.9.0",

    "react-dom": "^16.9.0"

},

"devDependencies": {

    "babel-loader": "^8.0.6",

    "@babel/core": "^7.6.0",

    "@babel/preset-react": "^7.0.0",

    "@babel/register": "^7.6.0",

    "webpack": "^4.19.1",

    "webpack-cli": "^3.3.2"

},
```

4. Alright. Once we have our dependencies setup correctly, let's write some code now. Here's our index.js file:

```
index.js
require("@babel/register")( {
presets: [ "@babel/preset-react" ]
} )
require( "./src/server" )
```

This would be the entry point of our script. You can see that we're using @babel/register package directly in the script file. This allows us to use JSX inside our node scripts directly.

5. Although babel could be configured via .babelrc to parse the server files as well, we'll just keep it simple right now and go with the minimal approach.

Alright, once our index.js file is setup, let's see the server.js file:

```
// server.js
const express = require("express")
const app = express()
const React = require("react")
const { renderToString } = require("react-dom/server")
app.get('/*', (req, res) => {
constjsx = <div>Hello</div>
constreactDom = renderToString(jsx)
res.send(template(reactDom))
});
app.listen(1337)
function template(reactDom) {
  return `
<!DOCTYPE html>
<html>
<head>
<meta charset="utf-8">
<title>React SSR</title>
</head>
<body>
<div id="root">${reactDom}</div>
</body>
</html>
`
}
```

Okay! Let's break down what is happening in this file:

1. Firstly, we require the necessary modules, the express module, and the react module.

2. We also import react-dom but notice that instead of just react-dom, we actually include react-dom/server.

3. This gives us access to the method called renderToString, which does what the namesays. Instead of rendering the host tree (the vDOM representation in JS) to the actual DOM, we render it to a simple string.

4. Finally, we send the response back to the client using res. send.

5. Notice we're using the template function to inject the constructed string into the response.

And once we start the server using node index.js, you could see that we get the correct response:

Figure 5.4

In the preceding screenshot, you can see that we get **Hello** sent by server which is actually running React code:

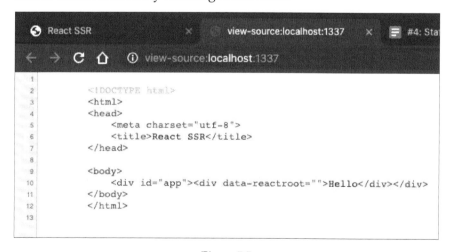

Figure 5.5

And once you see the source code of the page, as shown in the preceding screenshot, you'll see that this is actually sent by the server, and not rendered by the client.

Writing more components

We've done our basic Hello World with React SSR above, which got us into server-side rendering for the first time using React. Let's add some more components. Let's start with the Home page and About page:

```
// Home.js

const React = require('react')

function Home(props) {

return <div className="home">

<h2>Hello, this is homepage! Go to <a href="/about">About</a></h2>

</div>

}

module.exports = Home
```

And the About.js page:

```
const React = require('react')

function About(props) {

   return <div className="about">

<h2>This is the about page</h2>

</div>

}

module.exports = About
```

But do you see the problem above? How do we link them to each other, that is, when you click that link on the homepage, the about page should open? Similarly, when you directly visit/about the endpoint, it should directly serve that particular page. Let's do some routing.

Routing in SSR

Routing is one of the most important aspects of a web app these days, especially if it is a bit complex. It allows you to serve different content on different URL paths.

Let's start by installing the react-router package, which would help us to implement the routing.

npm install react-router-dom --save

Once you do that, we're good to make some changes. Let's change our server.js file a bit:

```
// server.js

const express = require("express")

const app = express()

const React = require("react")

constReactDOMServer = require("react-dom/server")

const { StaticRouter, Switch, Route } = require("react-router-dom")

const Home = require('./components/Home')

const About = require('./components/About')

app.get('/*', (req, res) => {

constjsx = <StaticRouter>

<Switch>

<Route path="/" component={Home} exact={true} />

<Route path="/about" component={About} exact={true} />

</Switch>

</StaticRouter>

constreactDom = ReactDOMServer.renderToString(jsx)

res.send(template(reactDom))

});

app.listen(1337)

function template(reactDom) {

  return `

<!DOCTYPE html>
```

```
<html>

<head>

<meta charset="utf-8">

<title>React SSR</title>

</head>

<body>

<div id="root">${reactDom}</div>

</body>

</html>

    `

}
```

Alright! Let's see what changed here:

- We included the StaticRouter, Switch and Route modules from the react-router-dom package.

- StaticRouter is a simple router in which the location is never changed. This is okay because we're rendering the React string on the server anyway, and there's no user interaction involved.

- Then we defined the Switch to match the first route, and then the Route which contains additional information on which component to display on which particular route.

If we visit the page right now, it willshow us the homepage:

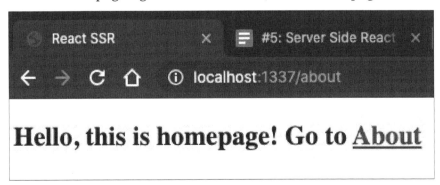

Figure 5.6

But if you go to /aboutthe route, it'll still show the same homepage component only, as shown in the following screenshot:

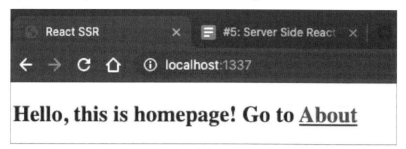

Figure 5.7

The preceding screenshot still shows the Home component being rendered. Why is that? See closely, our StaticRouter, although static, still needs to know the correct location in order to parse the proper route. We are missing the location prop on a static router. Also, for express, req.url gives us the requested path (that is,/about or / or /test) which is what we need to feed into our StaticRouter. Let's make the following change in the server.js file:

```
<StaticRouter location={req.url}>

<Switch>

<Route path="/" component={Home} exact={true} />

<Route path="/about" component={About} exact={true} />

</Switch>

</StaticRouter>
```

So we just added location={req.url} to our StaticRouter. Once we do this, now if you go to /about directly, we'll be served with /about component:

Figure 5.8

In the preceding screenshot, we see that our problem is fixed. It correctly renders the About component on the correct URL path. So far, so good. But we can still do better than this.

Client-Side React

React is aclient-side library. However, in the above SSR react, we've seen that we could write React-like markup on a server and send it to our client machine using a static router-based system. But in the process, we lost the actual "React" code on the frontend. Let's bring it back.

Let's create another file called client.js, and write the following code inside it:

```
import React from 'react'

import ReactDOM from 'react-dom'

import Home from './components/Home'

import About from './components/About'

import { BrowserRouter as Router, Route, Switch } from 'react-router-dom'

constjsx = (

<Router>

<Switch>

<Route path="/" component={Home} exact={true} />

<Route path="/about" component={About} exact={true} />

</Switch>

</Router>

)

const app = document.getElementById('root')

ReactDOM.hydrate(jsx, app)
```

We would place this file with the server.js file. And just to be clear on the file structure, here are all the files organized till now:

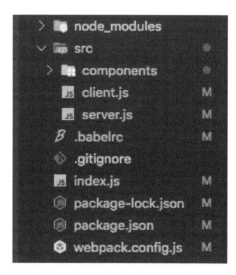

Figure 5.9

The preceding screenshot shows the file structure organized in the project. What you would've seen in the preceding code, is that we're using something called ReactDOM.hydrate instead of ReactDOM.render, we would come to this later in this section.

First, let us set up other things. We would also modify our server. js file to include our client.js file. This is how the server.js file should look finally:

```
const express = require("express")

const app = express()

const React = require("react")

constReactDOMServer = require("react-dom/server")

const { StaticRouter, Switch, Route } = require("react-router-dom")

const Home = require('./components/Home')

const About = require('./components/About')

app.use(express.static(path.resolve(__dirname, '../dist')))

app.get('/*', (req, res) => {

console.log(req.url)

constjsx = <StaticRouter location={req.url}>

<Switch>

<Route path="/" component={Home} exact={true} />
```

```
<Route path="/about" component={About} exact={true} />

</Switch>

</StaticRouter>

constreactDom = ReactDOMServer.renderToString(jsx)

res.send(template(reactDom))

});

app.listen(1337)

function template(reactDom) {

    return `

<!DOCTYPE html>

<html>

<head>

<meta charset="utf-8">

<title>React SSR</title>

</head>

<body>

<div id="root">${reactDom}</div>

<script src="./app.bundle.js"></script>

</body>

</html>

    `

}
```

Focus on lines in bold. Firstly, in the express server, we're configuring to serve our static files (that is, the client-side bundle file which we created above).

Then we included the script itself in the HTML response.

ReactDOM.hydrate

Instead of making use of ReactDOM.render, we're making use of ReactDOM.hydrate. ReactDOM.hydrate, as the name says, just *hydrates* the existing layout, it doesn't create the layout and replaces it in DOM. ReactDOM.hydrate knows that the layout string is coming from the server, so it just needs to sync the client-side JS (i.e. events and listeners) with the coming server-side HTML code. Hence, we make use of the hydrate method.

One interesting thing here to note is that ReactDOM.hydrate expects the layout you provide on the frontend (in client.js) to be close to that coming from the backend (server.js), otherwise it'll create problems for you.

Finally, let's set up webpack for frontend so that we canmake use of the import/export syntax and actually use React on the frontend.

We already installed webpack earlier, so just go ahead and create a webpack.config.js file like this:

```
const path = require('path')

module.exports = {

  mode: 'development',

devtool: 'source-map',

  entry: {

    app: './src/client.js',

  },

  module: {

    rules: [

      {

        test: /\.jsx?$/,

        exclude: /(node_modules|bower_components)/,

        loader: "babel-loader",

}

    ],

  },

  output: {

    path: path.resolve(__dirname, 'dist'),

    filename: '[name].bundle.js',

  }

}
```

Alright! Let's quickly look at what's going on in the webpack config file:

- We're setting up an entry point as the src/client.js file.
- We only have a single rule, whenever you see a JS or JSX file, let babel-loader handle it.
- Babel loader would be using our .babelrc file which we'll create next.
- Finally, spit out the file inside the dist directory with the name app.bundle.js ([name] is replaced by an app, that is, the key of the entry point).

And this is how our .babelrc file would look like:

```
{
"presets": [
"@babel/preset-react"
],
"plugins": ["@babel/plugin-syntax-dynamic-import"]
}
```

Remember, we've already installed this stuff before, so we could directly use it. Finally, let's go to package.json and create two scripts:

```
"scripts": {
  "server": "nodemonindex.js",
  "client": "webpack --watch --progress"
 }
```

Here, we're defining twoscripts, one is for starting an express server, and the second one is for building our client-side changes (they need to be compiled by webpack/babel before the browser can read them).

Fire up two different terminals and run npm run server in the first one and npm run client in the second one.

Finally, visit http://localhost:1337 again and see the source code:

```
<!DOCTYPE html>
<html>
<head>
    <meta charset="utf-8">
    <title>React SSR</title>
</head>

<body>
    <div id="root"><div class="home" data-reactroot=""><h2>
    <script src="./app.bundle.js"></script>
</body>
</html>
```

Figure 5.10

The preceding screenshot shows that now we include the JS required for the React code to run on the frontend:

```
←  →  C  ⌂    ⓘ localhost:1337/app.bundle.js

/******/ (function(modules) { // webpackBootstrap
/******/          // The module cache
/******/          var installedModules = {};
/******/
/******/          // The require function
/******/          function __webpack_require__(moduleId) {
/******/
/******/                  // Check if module is in cache
/******/                  if(installedModules[moduleId]) {
/******/                          return installedModules[module
/******/                  }
/******/                  // Create a new module (and put it int
/******/                  var module = installedModules[moduleId
/******/                          i: moduleId,
/******/                          l: false,
/******/                          exports: {}
/******/                  };
/******/
/******/                  // Execute the module function
/******/                  modules[moduleId].call(module.exports,
/******/
/******/                  // Flag the module as loaded
/******/                  module.l = true;
```

Figure 5.11

See the preceding screenshot;it shows the contents of app.bundle.js file. Great! So how do we use it now? Well, you could see that we're already sharing components folder between the client.js and server.js file, so whatever change we make once is rendered again in both the spaces.

So let's go ahead and instead of a direct anchor link to about page, let's do it with React Router, which would provide a seamless experience to the user when the user clicks on the hyperlink.

Update the Home.js file to:

```
// Home.js
const React = require('react')
const { Link } = require('react-router-dom')


function Home(props) {
return <div className="home">
<h2>Hello, this is homepage! Go to <Link to="/about">About</Link></h2>
</div>
}
module.exports = Home
```

Now, when you visit the homepage and click on the about link, it would not reload the page like before and navigate you without reloading to the /about page route. Similarly, if you land directly to /about page, the server would fetch you the contents of only /about page, and that is again, visible to you in the source code.

That's server-side rendering for you!

Fetching data

Although SSR with react is great, oftentimes you'll face difficulties with certain things because some things are only available in the browser environment and some things are only available in the node environment. One of those things is how to fetch data.

Let's make use of the package called isomorphic-fetch which allows us to use fetch in both the environments:

npm install isomorphic-fetch --save

Now, let's modify our Home.js file to look something like this:

```
// Home.js
const React = require('react')

const { Link } = require('react-router-dom')

require('isomorphic-fetch')

const { useEffect, useState } = React

function Home(props) {

const [data, setData] = useState(null)

useEffect(() => {

fetch('https://jsonplaceholder.typicode.com/posts/1').then(data =>data.json())

.then(data =>setData(data))

}, [])

if(!data) return <p>Loading...</p>

return <div className="home">

<h2>{data.title}</h2>

<p>{data.body}</p>

<Link to="/about">About</Link>

</div>

}

module.exports = Home
```

Notice here;we're using hooks. Since theuseEffect hook runs after the component ismounted, the code inside it is not executed on the server anyway. So we could've just used fetch without the isomorphic-fetch library, but still, we'll keep using it for now.

Then we finally grab the data and display it on the client-side:

Figure 5.12

The preceding screenshot shows how we're fetching the data on the client-side. So far, it looks good too. But can we do even better? How about fetching the data on the server side (in the Node environment) itself and then sending it to the client? Servers are powerful computers and can implement strong caching for commonly used resources, and could speed up things a lot. However, it starts becoming a pain with syncing server-side state and client-side state, as we'll see now.

Fetching data on the server

So the idea is that we'll expose whatever data a particular component wants througha property, and then we'll resolve all the promises and data fetching before we actually render the JSX to string. Finally, we'll somehow sync up the state and react code. Let's see how we would do this briefly. Let us see the updated Home.js file. Bear with me for a moment:

```
// Home.js

const React = require('react')

const { Link } = require('react-router-dom')

require('isomorphic-fetch')

const { useEffect, useState } = React

function Home(props) {

const [data, setData] = useState(process.env.BROWSER&&window.
```

```
componentsData[Home.name])
useEffect(() => {
if(!data) {
fetch('https://jsonplaceholder.typicode.com/posts/1').then(data =>data.json())
.then(data =>setData(data))
}
}, [])
if(!data) return <p>Loading...</p>
return <div className="home">
<h1>This is home page</h1>
<h2>{data.title}</h2>
<p>{data.body}</p>
<Link to="/about">About</Link>
</div>
}

Home.asyncData = 'https://jsonplaceholder.typicode.com/posts/1'
module.exports = Home
```

Let's understand what the preceding code does with the following points:

- Alright. So here, we've added some checks if the data is already available with us or not.

- We, first of all, check whether we're in the browser environment or not using process.env.BROWSER (we'll configure this in webpack soon).

- If the browser, we want to load the state from the global window object (we would set this up).

- Home.name gives us "Home", that is, the name of the function.

We've also added asyncData property to the Home component, which we'll use later to pre-fetch data on the server.

Let's update the About.js file as well:

```
const React = require('react')
```

```
const { Link } = require('react-router-dom')

const { useState, useEffect } = React

function About(props) {

const [data, setData] = useState(process.env.BROWSER&&window.
componentsData[About.name])

useEffect(() => {

if(!data) {

fetch('https://jsonplaceholder.typicode.com/posts/2').then(data =>data.json())

.then(data =>setData(data))

}

}, [])

if(!data) return <p>Loading...</p>

    return <div className="about">

<h1>This is home page</h1>

<h2>{data.title}</h2>

<p>{data.body}</p>

<Link to="/">Home</Link>

</div>

}

About.asyncData = 'https://jsonplaceholder.typicode.com/posts/2'

module.exports = About
```

Similar to Home.js, we're fetching more data in About.js file too. Also, we have an asyncData prop attached to About component which we'll use later.

Also, we need access to process.env.BROWSER variable when webpack is building our scripts, so we'll add that in the webpack.config.js file. This is how our webpack.config.js file would finally look like:

```
const path = require('path')

const webpack = require('webpack')

module.exports = {

    mode: 'development',

devtool: 'source-map',
```

```
entry: {
   app: './src/client.js',
},
module: {
   rules: [
      {
         test: /\.jsx?$/,
         exclude: /(node_modules|bower_components)/,
         loader: "babel-loader",
}
   ],
},
output: {
   path: path.resolve(__dirname, 'dist'),
   filename: '[name].bundle.js',
},
plugins: [
new webpack.DefinePlugin({
'process.env': {
 'BROWSER': 'true',
}
})
]
}
```

Once this is done, let's see what changes we have to make in the server.js file:

```
const express = require("express")

const app = express()

const React = require("react")

const path = require('path')

constReactDOMServer = require("react-dom/server")
```

```
const { StaticRouter, Switch, Route } = require("react-router-dom")

const Home = require('./components/Home')

const About = require('./components/About')

require('isomorphic-fetch')

app.use(express.static(path.resolve(__dirname, '../dist')))

app.get('/*', (req, res) => {

const components = [Home, About]

constasyncData = {}

const promises = components.map(c => ({

link: c.asyncData,

name: c.name

})).filter(item =>item.link).map(item => {

return fetch(item.link).then(data =>data.json()).then(json => {

asyncData[item.name] = json

})

})

constjsx = <StaticRouter location={req.url}>

<Switch>

<Route path="/" component={Home} exact={true} />

<Route path="/about" component={About} exact={true} />

</Switch>

</StaticRouter>

Promise.all(promises).then(() => {

constreactDom = ReactDOMServer.renderToString(jsx)

res.send(template(reactDom, asyncData))

})

})

app.listen(1337)

function template(reactDom, data) {

    return `

<!DOCTYPE html>
```

```
<html>

<head>

<meta charset="utf-8">

<title>React SSR</title>

</head>

<body>

<div id="root">${reactDom}</div>

<script>

window.componentsData = ${JSON.stringify(data)}

</script>

<script src="./app.bundle.js"></script>

</body>

</html>
```

    `

}

Okay! So what's happening in this file?

- First, we collect all components together in an array called components.

- Then we create an array of Promises. Finally, this array would contain multiple unresolved fetch requests.

- Here, we start with our components array and create a new array of objects with the link to fetch (the asyncData link) and the name of the component (in JavaScript, Function.name gives you the name of that function)

- We use the name to link it to a specific component.

- Finally, we filter this array to remove elements that did not have any async data to be fetched.

- When we're done with it, we do a final map where we fetch all the data and return the promise. See, in the fetch request, I'm assigning item.name as the key in asyncData object, and json (the result returned from a remote server), as the value in asyncData object.

- At this point, promises contain all fetch requests going on in parallel. Now, we want to wait for all the fetch requests before sending data back to the client.

- Hence, we wait for all Promises to resolve using Promise.all. Once that is done, we construct our ReactDOM and send it to the client.

- For the client, we do a normal hydrate, but we also send the client state using a script tag, as seen at the endof the HTML section.

And once we do that, you would be able to see that there is no *fetching* of data on the frontend. The page loads up immediately, and there's no fetch request in the DevTools because all the data is already available for us from the server:

Figure 5.13

In the preceding screenshot , you can see there's no data request to the remote server because it is already available with the frontend when the server sendsthe data. Awesome! But we have some problems even after this approach:

Our constructed tree is now inconsistent between server and client renders. This is because, when the react code is rendered on the server, it doesn't know about process.env.BROWSER hence it doesn't prefill the state variable, and hence it usesthat Loading segment. On the client-side, however, when React rehydrates the data, it already has the data in the global scope, so it rehydrates it with the actual data, hence creating an inconsistency, which React reports to us as well in the console:

Figure 5.14

- In this preceding screenshot, you can see that React complains about DOM mismatch, what it expects versus what server actually sent.
- Another thing, we're fetching the async data of all components, although we just need to fetch the async data of the active component.
- We are also not handling the nested component problem, where a lot of nested components need async data from each other.
- A single component might need multiple async data from various sources;we don't handle that either.

Conclusion

Remember, we discussed back that SSR with React is not a cakewalk;you need to handle a lot of edge cases for it to work for you properly. Hence, it is not feasible to fix each and every small detail yourself. Hence, we'll be using certain frameworks that would abstract a lot of these details from us and allow us to focus more on the code rather than on these small details to be implemented. In the coming chapters, we'll be talking about Next.js, one such popular framework for React to create production-ready server-side rendering applications.

Questions

1. How does Server Side Rendering differ from normal client-side React code?

2. Is PHP a server-side rendering language? Why/Why not?

3. What does Babel do?

4. What is the difference between StaticRouter and Normal Router?

5. What is the difference between ReactDOM.render and ReactDOM.hydrate?

6. What do you mean by isomorphic JavaScript?

CHAPTER 6

Introduction to Next.js

In the last chapter, we learned a lot about getting started with server-side rendering with React from bare-bones and saw how much tooling it could take just to get to simple results synchronized between client and server machines. Now, let's get into Next.js, see what it is and why it is a great option to go about.

Structure

- What is Next.js
- Installation
- Default settings
- Pages in Next.js
- Static assets
- Routing
- Components
- CSS

Objective

This chapter aims to introduce you to Next.js, which is a server-side rendering framework built for React. Next.js is going to simplify a lot of workflow for you as a developer so that more energy could be spent on the application logic and purpose and less energy on the infrastructure part. We'll learn about what it is, how to set it up and work with it in an effective manner.

What is Next.js?

Next.js is a framework for building server-side applications with React. A framework provides a lot of things out of the box. Next.js provides solutions to routing, managing pages, server-side rendering, caching, etc. out of the box and is extremely easy to set up.

You could compare Next.js ease-of-setup that to of create-react-app. Just like how cumbersome it is to set up a React project manually, in the last chapter, we saw that it is equally cumbersome to set up a React SSR project manually. Next.js to the rescue!

Why Next.js?

From their official site, here are some points explaining why it is a good choice:

1. Server Rendering: This is the main reason for using Next.js.

2. Static Export: This means that you could generate a static bundle of your website (not possible in every case) if you want within a few clicks and commands.

3. CSS-in-JS: CSS in JS is a popular technique in which people write styles directly in JS. Some people frown upon the practice, but more or less, the community appreciates it and has developed numerous solutions around it. Next.js supports all of them

4. Zero setup: It is as simple as create-react-app when setting it up. We'll be up and ready with our Hello World with Next.js within a few minutes.

5. Fully extensible: You can control the babel and webpack configuration. And once you're able to control that, you can pretty much control every fine detail of your project.

6. Ready for production: It is an open-source and highly optimized framework which is quite mature now for creating production-ready apps with React.

These are some of the many reasons you could go with Next.js if you're willing to opt into an SSR solution using React.

Installation

Let's begin by setting up Next.js for our project.

1. Create a directory named react-ssr-next

2. Using the command line, cd into that directory

3. Run the following commands:

   npminit -y

   npm install react react-dom next --save

   These commands basically setup your package.json file and install the required dependencies. Did you notice that we only needed threepackages in total? The react, react-dom, and the next package!

4. Finally, go ahead and make these changes to your package.json file's scripts section, so it looks like this:

   "scripts": {

     "dev": "next",

     "build": "next build",

     "start": "next start"

   }

   So, your package.json file would look more or less like the following (your version numbers might be different):

   {

     "name": "nextjs",

     "version": "1.0.0",

     "main": "index.js",

     "scripts": {

     "dev": "next",

     "build": "next build",

     "start": "next start"

     },

```
"keywords": [],

"author": "",

"license": "ISC",

"description": "",

"dependencies": {

  "next": "^9.1.1",

  "react": "^16.9.0",

  "react-dom": "^16.9.0"

}

}
```

5. Now, we would create a pages directory inside the root folder. This is required by the Next.js framework.

6. Let's go ahead and do npm run dev in the same directory.

It'll spin up Next.js processes. But because our pages directory is empty, we don't have any page to serve yet.

Anyway, it'll give us a URL with a bunch of information: http://localhost:3000:

```
⚡ dev  ~/nextjs  npm run dev

> nextjs@1.0.0 dev /Users/dev/nextjs
> next

[ wait ]  starting the development server ...
[ info ]  waiting on http://localhost:3000 ...
[ ready ] compiled successfully - ready on http://localhost:3000
Attention: Next.js now collects completely anonymous telemetry re
This information is used to shape Next.js' roadmap and prioritize
You can learn more, including how to opt-out if you'd not like to
iting the following URL:
https://nextjs.org/telemetry

[ wait ]  compiling ...
[ ready ] compiled successfully - ready on http://localhost:3000
```

Figure 6.1

In the preceding screenshot, we can see that running npm run dev starts a development Next.js server for us to use.

7. On navigating to localhost:3000 however, you'll see a 404 page. This is because our pages directory is empty, and Next. js doesn't serve anything yet.

Next.js defaults

At this point, we've Next.js set up correctly and running. With Next.js, to avoid messing around with a lot of configuration in the beginning, Next.js locks down certain default configuration. Let's look at them one by one.

Pages

We created the pages folder above. That folder is just not a random name I gave from my side. Whatever filename you create inside that folder; it is created as a route in your application! Let's start with simple index.js page, which is the root page of the application:

In the pages/index.js file, let's write the following simple React component:

```
// pages/index.js
export default () =><h1>Hello World</h1>
```

That's it! Go ahead and refresh the localhost:3000 page (it'll refresh automatically anyway because hot reloading is on), and there we have it:

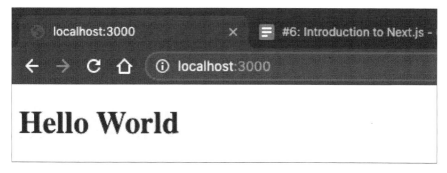

Figure 6.2

In the preceding screenshot, we could see that we successfully got a Hello World output on the screen using Next.js.

Upon looking at the source code, we'll see the following:

```
<!DOCTYPE html><html><head><meta charSet="utf-8"/><meta
name="viewport" content="width=device-width,minimum-scale=1,initial-
scale=1"/><meta name="next-head-count" content="2"/><link rel="preload"
href="/_next/static/development/pages/index.js?ts=1569413352906"
as="script"/><link rel="preload" href="/_next/static/development/pages/_
app.js?ts=1569413352906" as="script"/><link rel="preload" href="/_next/
static/runtime/webpack.js?ts=1569413352906" as="script"/><link
rel="preload" href="/_next/static/runtime/main.js?ts=1569413352906"
as="script"/></head><body><div id="__next"><h1>Hello World</h1></
div><script src="/_next/static/development/dll/dll_397dc449097af0b4e992.
js?ts=1569413352906"></script><script id="__NEXT_DATA__"
type="application/json">{"dataManager":"[]","props":{"pageProps":{}},"p
age":"/","query":{},"buildId":"development","nextExport":true,"autoExpo
rt":true}</script><script async="" data-next-page="/" src="/_next/static/
development/pages/index.js?ts=1569413352906"></script><script async=""
data-next-page="/_app" src="/_next/static/development/pages/_app.
js?ts=1569413352906"></script><script src="/_next/static/runtime/webpack.
js?ts=1569413352906" async=""></script><script src="/_next/static/runtime/
main.js?ts=1569413352906" async=""></script></body></html>
```

A lot of this is just the development stuff and hot reloading scripts. But we could clearly see that Hello World markup is rendered in source code, and not created on the fly using client-side JavaScript. Hey, that's server-side rendering!

Let's create an about.js file now:

```
// pages/about.js

constAboutMe = () => {

return (

<div id="about-me">

<h1>Hey Guys!</h1>

<p>My name is Mehul and I'm the author of this book.</p>

<p>This book covers React and stuff</p>

<p>I like React</p>

</div>

)

}

export default AboutMe
```

And that's basically it! Save the file and visit localhost:3000/about and you'll see the following page:

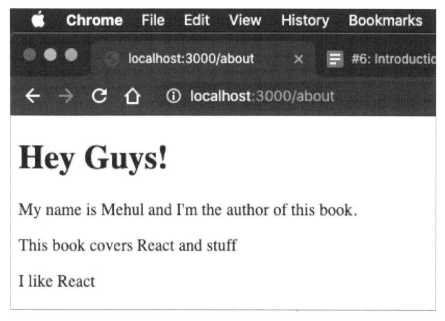

Figure 6.3

The precedingpage shows our content which we wrote as a React component in the file about.js without any extra configuration from our end. Next.js takes care of the routing under the hood.

Hot code reloading

You see when we make changes to our code, and the next server is running (using npm run dev command), we don't have to go to the browser and refresh the changes manually. Next.js automatically communicates with the filesystem to detect whether there has been any change and if there has been, it'll build it again and push the message to the browser to fetch new changes and update accordingly.

This is offered out of the box when you're using Next.

Static file serving

Next.js can also serve your static files (images, videos, fonts, and so on) using a special directory name. Go ahead and create a directory named static at the root of the project. Anything you place under this directory is served on /static/ route.

Let's try to put an image in the public/static folder. The final folder structure looks like the following:

Figure 6.4

The preceding screenshot shows whatthe file structure should look like.

Once you do that, you should be able to navigate to localhost:3000/static/profile.jpeg:

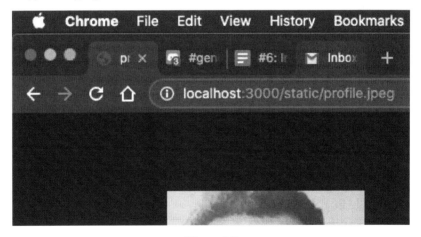

Figure 6.5

You could place all your static assets in the static directory in your project.

In the earlier versions of Next, you had to place all the static assets inside the static folder in the root directory. Now, you can place anything you want inside the public folder, and it'll be available at your root URL path. But still, we'll store static assets in public/static path to be clear what assets are static and what are not.

Routing

In Next.js, routing is a cakewalk, at least the basic routing. Above, we saw a very basic demonstration of how routing could work - just by creating JavaScript files inside a folder. But we need to *link* these pages together as well. How would we go about that?

Of course, we could do linking using our regular anchor tags, but remember, just like raw React SSR, this would perform a full redirect, and we don't want that simply because we have the ability to perform a background fetch of updated data and update the UI using React, that's the whole point of using React! So, let's use Link from Next.js.

Link

Link API from Next.js allows you to perform the navigation just like we did with the Link component from the react-router-dom package.

Here's how to use it. We'll update our index.js file to link it to our about page:

```
// pages/index.js
import Link from 'next/link'
const Home = () => {
return <div id="home">
<h1>This is a nice homepage</h1>
<p>Click <Link href="/about"><a>here</a></Link> to go to about page</p>
</div>
}
export default Home
```

Here's what's going on:

- Firstly, we import the Link component to use.
- Next, we surround the text we want to act as a hyperlink with the Link component.
- Notice we're giving href attribute to the Link component, and inside that, we're again making use of anchor tag. This is important, and we'll come to this later.

- Finally, in the href attribute, we're passing the link we want to navigate to. Let's see what output it generates:

```
tic/development/pages/index.js?ts=1569426740343" as="script"/><link rel="preload" href="/_next
xt/static/runtime/webpack.js?ts=1569426740343" as="script"/><link rel="preload" href="/_next/s
"><h1>This is a nice homepage</h1><p>Click <a href="/about">here</a> to go to about page</p></
/dll/dll_397dc449097af0b4e992.js?ts=1569426740343"></script><script id="__NEXT_DATA__" type="a
ldId":"development","nextExport":true,"autoExport":true}</script><script async="" data-next-pa
```

Figure 6.6

The preceding screenshot shows how the Link component gets transpiled to the regular anchor tag in HTML on render.

- Great! We can see that our hyperlink is there in the source code. But using the Link component, Next.js also handles the client-side navigation using the HTML5 history API automatically without us ever touching any code.

- Now when you click on the **About**link, it'll seamlessly navigate to the about page.

Now, let's explore more about this Link component and how it is different from the one we're used to seeing with react-router-dom.

Link is just HoC

If you're coming from the react-router-dom,Link component, you might confuse this Link with that one. In react-router-dom, you could actually pass props to that component itself, and it'll turn into a hyperlink and use those props (like className, onClick, and so on). But with the Link API provided by Next.js, it is just a Higher Order Component, that is, it just glues your child component to the click event of history API changes. It won't pass down the props you supply to it, to the children, and hence you have to make whatever changes you want to make on the child, and not on the Link component.

For example, consider the following code snippet. This is wrong way of assigning a class to the anchor tag:

```
<p>Click <Link href="/about" className="mylink"><a>here</a></Link> to go to about page</p>
```

In fact, if you run the precedingcode, you'll see that you don't get myLink class attached to your anchor tag.

This is the correct way to add class to that anchor tag:

```
<p>Click <Link href="/about"><a className="mylink">here</a></Link> to go to about page</p>
```

More on Link

The Link component basically attaches an onClick event to its child. So, if the child supports onClick event, Link would work. Consider the following case:

```
<Link href="/about"><imgsrc="/static/profile.jpeg" /></Link>
```

In this case, Link would work correctly, and the navigation would happen, but you won't get any atags with the href attribute set in the HTML markup, which might be bad for SEO.

Hence, you should wrap the img tag above in an anchor tag.

If you want Next.js to display the href attribute on tags other than anchor tag (for debugging purposes), you can pass passHref attribute to the Link component like this:

```
<Link href="/about" passHref>

<imgsrc="/static/profile.jpeg" />

</Link>
```

This would render the following markup:

```
<imgsrc="/static/profile.jpeg" href="/about"/>
```

This is good for debugging purposes when you want to find out what is the link page is going to be redirected on clicking that particular element.

Next.js components

Pages are fine, but what about reusable code pieces? We can obviously create component files which could be included in other pages. Let's create a directory called **components**, but remember, unlike pages or static, this time the name of the directory is not important. Here's a simple example:

```
// components/Header.js

import Link from 'next/link'

const Header = () => (

<header>

<Link href="/">
```

```
<a>Home</a>

</Link>

<Link href="/about">

<a>About</a>

</Link>

</header>

)

export default Header
```

Now, let's use this Header component we created above in the index. js file:

```
// pages/index.js

import Link from 'next/link'

import Header from '../components/Header'

const Home = () => {

return <div id="home">

<Header />

<h1>This is a nice homepage</h1>

<p>Click <Link href="/about" passHref><imgsrc="/static/profile.jpeg" /></Link>
to go to about page</p>

</div>

}

export default Home
```

About.js file:

```
// pages/about.js

import Header from '../components/Header'

constAboutMe = () => {               ·

return (

<div id="about-me">

<Header />

<h1>Hey Guys!</h1>

<p>My name Is Mehul and I'm the author of this book.</p>
```

```
<p>This book covers React and stuff</p>

<p>I like React</p>

</div>

)

}

export default AboutMe
```

And the file structure looks like this:

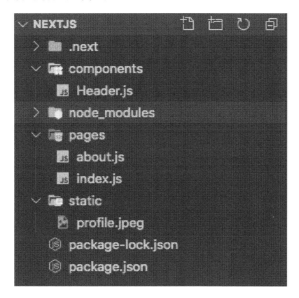

Figure 6.7

The preceding screenshot shows whatthe file structure should look like at this moment.

Now you'll see that we're able to reuse the Header component on both the pages (About and Home).

Also, note that, as said above, components are just a choice, you could name this folder anything you like and still use it (as we're using a relative path to address the folder).

Next.js + CSS

There are a bunch of ways to use CSS with the Next.js framework, and you would always use CSS in applications these days. Let's explore some of the common ways to do that.

Styled JSX

This method requires you to write your CSS directly in the JSX template. Let's look at an example first. Let's modify our Header component to include some styles:

```
// Header.js

import Link from 'next/link'

const Header = () => (

<header>

<style jsx>{

  `

  header {

  padding: 20px;

  background: #1e1e1e;

  border-bottom: 1px solid black;

  font-size: 30px;

  }

a {

color: white;

margin-right: 30px;

}

  `

  }</style>

<Link href="/">

<a>Home</a>

</Link>

<Link href="/about">

<a>About</a>

</Link>

</header>

)

export default Header
```

This generates the following mockup:

Figure 6.8

Just like the code describes, the preceding screenshot shows the output we expected.

Now, let's look at the rendered HTML. When you see that, you'll see something like this:

```
▼<div id="home">
  ▼<header class="jsx-2373410506"> == $0
    <a class="jsx-2373410506" href="/">Home</a>
    <a class="jsx-2373410506" href="/about">
    About</a>
  </header>

header.jsx-2373410506 {
  padding: ▶ 20px;
  background: ▶ ☐#1e1e1
  border-bottom: ▶ 1px s
  font-size: 30px;
}
```

Figure 6.9

The preceding screenshot shows us the output DOM tree from the Chrome DevTools.

See that even though we didn't assign any class to our header/anchor elements, Next.js did that itself for us to locally scope the styles. This way, even if you have the same elements in different components, you can style them differently without worrying about style conflicts. This is extremely useful when you're targeting elements directly either through their tag names or through some use of very common classes (like "container", "block", and so on).

But what about the cases where you actually want to target global? For example, writing the same styles in the top file for it to have effects globally? For that, we could include the global attribute. Check the following example:

```
import Link from 'next/link'

const Header = () => (

<header>

<style jsx global>{

 `

  header {

  padding: 20px;

  background: #1e1e1e;

  border-bottom: 1px solid black;

  font-size: 30px;

  }

a {

color: white;

margin-right: 30px;

}

 `

 }</style>

<Link href="/">

<a>Home</a>

</Link>

<Link href="/about">

<a>About</a>

</Link>

</header>

)

export default Header
```

This is exactly the same example as above with the exception that now we have a global attribute in the style tag. Although the HTML part would still include syntax for custom scoping, the CSS part is now truly global, as you can see in the rendered output:

```
<body data-gr-c-s-loaded="true">
  ▼ <div id="__next">
    ▼ <div id="home">
      ▼ <header class="jsx-2373410506">
          <a class="jsx-2373410506" href="/">Home</a>
          <a class="jsx-2373410506" href="/about">About</a> ══
        </header>
```

```
element.style {
}

a {
    color: ■white;
    margin-right: 30px;
}

a:-webkit-any-link {
```

Figure 6.10

The preceding screenshot shows how the anchor tag is rendered by our Next.js code.

See, in the style section on the right, we have simply the anchor tag being targeted, instead of the long class name associated with it. This means we're targeting all the anchor tags on the page.

Importing CSS files

Honestly, for me, writing CSS directly inside JSX is a bit overwhelming, and I would like to keep it separated for clarity. Moreover, in separate files, you'll be able to get better syntax highlighting and error handling. Let's see how we can set up importing CSS files in our pages.

Unlike styled-jsx, CSS imports are not baked in Next.js by default just because there could be many ways to achieve this. Let's install the @ zeit/next-css package first. Follow the steps:

1. In your project root, do npmi @zeit/next-css --save

2. Now, we've to create a next.config.js file in the root directory of the project. Here's how the file would look like:

   // next.config.js

   constwithCSS = require('@zeit/next-css')

   module.exports = withCSS({})

3. Restart your dev server at this point

4. You could pass additional options in withCSS function, for example, using CSS modules

5. Once this is done, let's move our styles in a separate file

Here's how our Header.js component looks finally:

// components/Header/index.js

import Link from 'next/link'

```
import './style.css'
const Header = () => (
<header>
<Link href="/">
<a>Home</a>
</Link>
<Link href="/about">
<a className="special">About</a>
</Link>
</header>
)
export default Header
```

And here's how the style.css file would look like:

```
// components/Header/style.css
header {
padding: 20px;
background: #1e1e1e;
border-bottom: 1px solid black;
font-size: 30px;
}
a {
color: white;
  margin-right: 30px;
}
a.special {
color: yellow;
}
```

And this would produce the following output:

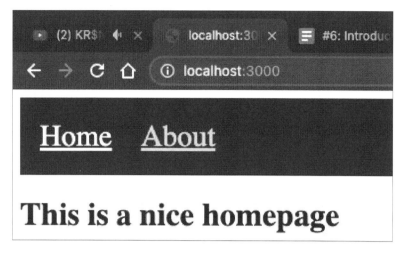

Figure 6.11

The preceding screenshot shows the output produced by the Header component file we just coded.

Also, there's a change in the file structure for the components directory. See below:

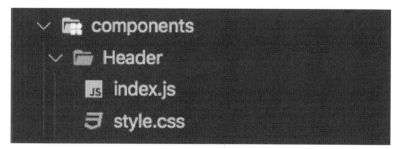

Figure 6.12

The preceding screenshot shows how the file structure looks right now.

Awesome! Let's use CSS modules now. We can switch the site's behaviour to use CSS modules, which means that the class names would be randomized so that there's no collision between the same class names in different components. Let's see how this is done. Change the next.config.js file to the following:

```
// next.config.js

constwithCSS = require('@zeit/next-css')
```

```
module.exports = withCSS({

cssModules: true

})
```

Once you do this and restart the server, you'll see that your About link is no longer yellow even though it has a special class in the HTML markup. This is because now you have CSS modules in place, and the class name "special" has been rewritten by the CSS module system. Now, in order to apply a class to a particular element, you have to use the imported styles. Change the Header.js file as follows:

```
import Link from 'next/link'

import css from './style.css'

const Header = () => (

<header>

<Link href="/">

<a>Home</a>

</Link>

<Link href="/about">

<a className={css.special}>About</a>

</Link>

</header>

)

export default Header
```

And this should work now! See the HTML markup, and it is a completely random class name. This is basically the webpack CSS loader, and you can customize it, even more, using the options present in webpack docs: https://github.com/webpack-contrib/css-loader.

Conclusion

This chapter introduced us to the Next.js framework and helped us understand some of its core concepts in order to get started with it and set up certain aspects of it.

We learned about what Next.js is, bootstrapping our first project with it and seeing under the hood how the response sent to the browser is truly rendered HTML.

In the next chapter, we'll see how we can work even more with this framework and dive deeper under the hood to see how Next.js works and how we can tweak the framework to our needs.

Questions

1. How does Next.js differ from running React on the server-side as we did in the last chapter?

2. Consider there's a component at pages/myroute/index.js. Would it be accessible at localhost:3000/myroute when running in development mode?

3. How do you host a file robots.txt on the root path, that is, at localhost:3000/robots.txt? Where do you place the file?

4. What is the difference between Link from Next.js and Link from react-router-dom?

5. List some ways to use CSS with your Next.js component.

CHAPTER 7

More with Next.js

In the last chapter, we learned about Next.js, what it is, and how to spin up a basic SSR React project with it very quickly. However, applications are often more complicated than that and require a lot of nits and grits to be handled. In this chapter, we'll explore some fine parts of Next.js and see how we can incorporate them into our code. This is important as most of the applications would sometimes need a custom tweak or changes according to their needs. Let's dive into it.

Structure

- Creating a Next.js project
- Introduction to Redux
- Setting up Redux with Next.js
- TypeScript + Next
- Creating API endpoints with Next.js
- Next.js custom files
- Dynamic routing

Objective

The objective of this chapter is to spend more time with Next. js framework as a whole to make ourselves comfortable with the ecosystem and spinning up some projects in Next.js from scratch exploring various Next.js concepts on the way.

Next.js application

In this chapter, let's create a Next.js app while discussing important concepts regarding the application. We'll create a login portal showing some custom values depending on what kind of user logged in. We'll start from the basics and learn and include technologies like Redux eventually. Let's start.

Getting project up

First things first, let's start with a fresh Next.js project now. It is simple, and we did it in the last chapter. Here are some key points we'll take care of this project:

- Now for this project, for now, we need a login page, a registration page, and a dashboard page.

- Let's keep our login page as our index page for simplicity.

- But before anything, let's switch to TypeScript for Next.js (just like we did with React earlier).

Switching to TypeScript

TypeScript has proven itself to be a very reliable method writing JavaScript on the scale, and almost every codebase after hitting a certain scale would suffer from the common JavaScript pitfalls like no type checking support. TypeScript comes very handily in this sense. It compiles down to JavaScript, at the same time allows us to use the best version of JavaScript for developers to write.

- To create a TypeScript project, let's use the create-next-app utility directly from npx

- Go to a directory where you want to set up your Next.js (or should we call it, Next.ts project

- Run the following command:

npx create-next-app --example with-typescript my-custom-app

- What this does is that it pulls the create-next-app package and runs it with the supplied arguments. It pulls an example repo that uses TypeScript and then creates our project with the name my-custom-app with all the npm install and package. json stuff already taken care of.

- Once you do that, open the project in your text editor.

This is how your file structure should look like right now:

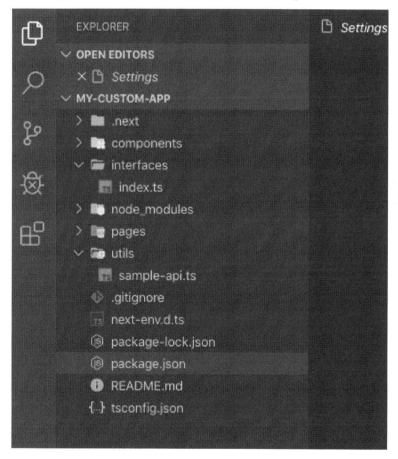

Figure 7.1

The preceding screenshot shows the file structure right now.

Start your application using npm run dev which would start a local development server at localhost:3000

Now, let's look at a state management tool called Redux.

Redux

Redux is a generic state management tool that could be used as one of the options with React. Redux basically centralizes the state and makes the flow of data unidirectional. Remember how we used Context API in the *State Management* chapter? Redux falls on very similar lines, just that it is an external dependency and comes with Redux DevTools and a bunch of other benefits.

Let's see how we can integrate Redux with Next.js and how to work with it in general. But before that, let's look at something called getInitialProps lifecycle in Next.js.

getInitialProps

In Next.js, getInitialProps is used to populate the props with some custom logic if you want to before the component is rendered. This method is executed on both the client and the server. Let's look at some code to understand in a better way. Let's modify the about.ts file present in our project:

```
// about.ts
import * as React from 'react'
import Link from 'next/link'
import Layout from '../components/Layout'
import { NextPage, NextPageContext } from 'next'
type Props = {
someprop: string
}
const AboutPage: NextPage<Props> = (props: Props) => (
<Layout title="About | Next.js + TypeScript Example">
<h1>About</h1>
<p>This is the about page</p>
```

```
<p>

<Link href="/">

<a>Go home {props.someprop}</a>

</Link>

</p>

</Layout>

)

AboutPage.getInitialProps = async ({pathname, query}: NextPageContext) => {

  console.log(pathname, query)

  return {

someprop: 'customvalue'

  }

}

export default AboutPage
```

The lines in bold are the changes we did in this file. Notice how we have added a function called getInitialProps to the AboutPage. This function runs before the component is mounted, as you can see, this function is supposed to return a Promise. Thus, you can do all sorts of async activity in it as well, as well as set up our Redux store (more on this later). Since this is coming out from Next.js, it is isomorphic and runs both on server and client.

In the browser it produces the following output:

Figure 7.2

The preceding screenshot shows the output from the browser.

And the console looks like the following:

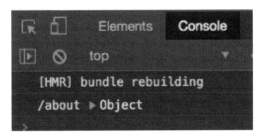

Figure 7.3

The preceding screenshot shows the output from the browser.

Okay. Let's start with our app now.

Creating App

Let's start with the index.ts page which would be our login page:

1. Here's a quick example of index.ts file we could use:

```
// pages/index.ts
import React, { useState } from 'react'
import { NextPage } from 'next'
import './styles.css'
const IndexPage: NextPage = () => {
  const [username, setUsername] = useState<string>('')
  const [password, setPassword] = useState<string>('')
  return (
<form method="POST">
<div className="box">
<h1>Login</h1>
<input type="text" placeholder="Username" className="field" value={username} onChange={e =>setUsername(e.target.value)} />

<input type="password" placeholder="Password" className="field" value={password} onChange={e =>setPassword(e.target.value)} />

<div className="btn">Sign In</div>
```

```
</div>
</form>
 )
}
export default IndexPage
```

The component above just creates a simple controlled Login form in React which we'll see soon.

2. The styles.css file associated with the index.js file should be:

```
// styles.css
* {
  margin: 0;
  padding: 0;
  box-sizing: border-box;
  outline: 0;
}
body {
  font-family: 'Open Sans', sans-serif;
  background: #3498db;
  margin: 0 auto 0 auto;
  width: 100%;
  text-align: center;
  margin: 20px 0px 20px 0px;
}
p {
  font-size: 12px;
  text-decoration: none;
  color: #ffffff;
}
h1 {
  font-size: 1.5em;
  color: #525252;
```

```css
}
.box {
  background: white;
  width: 300px;
  position: absolute;
  top: 50%;
  left: 50%;
  transform: translate(-50%, -50%);
  border-radius: 6px;
  padding: 20px;
  box-shadow: 0 0 5px black;
}
.field {
  background: #ecf0f1;
  border: #ccc 1px solid;
  border-bottom: #ccc 2px solid;
  padding: 8px;
  width: 100%;
  color: #AAA;
  margin-top: 10px;
  font-size: 1em;
  border-radius: 4px;
}
.btn {
  background: #2ecc71;
  width: 100%;
  cursor: pointer;
  padding: 5px 0;
  color: white;
  border-radius: 4px;
  border: #27ae60 1px solid;
```

```
    margin-top: 20px;

    font-weight: 800;

    font-size: 0.8em;

}

.btn:hover {

    background: #2CC06B;

}
```

Note that I'm importing styles.css from a different file, hence we need a custom next.config.js file as well in our project root directory (as discussed in the last chapter):

```
// next.config.js

const withCSS = require('@zeit/next-css')

module.exports = withCSS({})
```

And also install the @zeit/next-cssnpm module:

npmi @zeit/next-css -S

Once you do that, don't forget to restart the server.

This would give us a nice output of following:

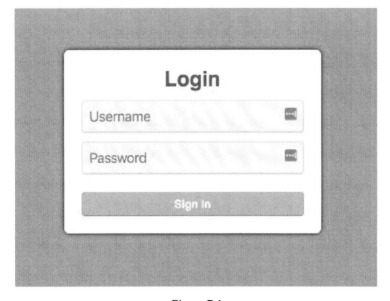

Figure 7.4

The preceding screenshot shows the output of the Login form we created above.

Notice how we're using the useState hook right now for managing the username and password for this component. And this is the right approach for this because we don't need to store this component's so local state into a redux store. Let's keep going.

Now we'll set up a quick backend in Next.js to receive the login and process it.

APIs using Next.js

When we spun out our TypeScript demo, you must have seen that there's a folder called api which was present under the pages folder. This folder is special. Prior to Next.js v9, we had to set up our own server for handling API calls. This was cumbersome as it is tiring to maintain 2 Node servers handling a single purpose. But now, Next.js natively supports handling API calls. We'll soon cover dynamic routing as well.

Delete whatever was present inside the api folder and create a new folder called login and within that create a file called index.ts. The contents of the following should look like the following:

```
// pages/api/login/index.ts
import { NextApiRequest, NextApiResponse } from 'next'
export default async (req: NextApiRequest, res: NextApiResponse) => {
  const { username, password } = req.body
  if(username === 'admin' && password === 'admin') {
    return res.json({
      status: 'ok',
      data: {
        name: 'Mehul Mohan',
        age: 21,
favQuote: 'Nobody cares about your feelings bro.'
      }
    })
```

```
}
   return res.json({ status: 'error', message: 'Invalid login' })
}
```

Alright! So, what's happening in this file?

- We created a file under pages/api/login/index.ts.

- In this file, we export a function instead of a React component. This is because this is our API endpoint and we are allowed to write logic here.

- There are two arguments which Next.js passes for us to work with. The first one is req (the request handler) and the second one is res (the response handler).

- The first parameter, req, contains all the relevant information about the current request hitting that particular endpoint. This might include the POST body data, authentication cookies, custom headers, and so on.

- The second parameter, res, is writable by you, the developer. This has methods to call which would, in turn, create an HTTP response under the hood which the API endpoint is supposed to send back to the client.

- If you have ever used Express with Node.js, this might seem very familiar.

- We, first of all, pull out the username and password from req. body. The body property on the req handler would contain whatever we send from the client to the server. Since we're expecting a JSON request, we can just destructure it directly.

- Once we get that, we check against the values.

- If both are admin, we authenticate (for now).

- If not, we send a custom error message.

- Note we're using the res.json() method to send back the response. If we look at the type declaration of NextApiResponse, we'll see that the following methods are supported on res object:

```
export declare type NextApiResponse<T = any> = ServerResponse& {
   /**
```

```
   * Send data `any` data in response
   */
   send: Send<T>;
   /**
   * Send data `json` data in response
   */
   json: Send<T>;
   status: (statusCode: number) =>NextApiResponse<T>;
};
```

- As the comments describe, send just sends the raw text back to the client.

- The json method takes the object, serializes it into a JSON string, sets appropriate Content-Type header, and sends it to the client.

- If you want a custom status code set as well (default is 200 OK), you can use the status method attached to it.

Let's update our index.tsx file of the homepage to send the data back to server API:

```
// pages/index.tsx
import React, { useState } from 'react'
import { NextPage } from 'next'
import './styles.css'
const IndexPage: NextPage = () => {
  const [username, setUsername] = useState<string>('')
  const [password, setPassword] = useState<string>('')
  async function submitForm() {
    const req = await fetch('/api/login', {
      method: 'POST',
      headers: {
        'Content-Type': 'application/json'
      },
      body: JSON.stringify({ username, password })
```

```
  })

  const json = await req.json()

  console.log(json)

  }

  return (

<form method="POST">

<div className="box">

<h1>Login</h1>

<input type="text" placeholder="Username" className="field"
value={username} onChange={e =>setUsername(e.target.value)} />

<input type="password" placeholder="Password" className="field"
value={password} onChange={e =>setPassword(e.target.value)} />

<div className="btn" onClick={submitForm}>Sign In</div>

</div>

</form>

  )

}

export default IndexPage
```

We added a new function called submitForm, which is fired when the Login button is clicked. And the result of the following is:

Incorrect login:

Figure 7.5

The preceding screenshot shows a representation of incorrect login done by the user.

Correct login:

Figure 7.6

The preceding screenshot shows a representation of the correct login done by the user.

Great! We just implemented our first API endpoint using Next.js. Let's go ahead and put this data in our Redux store now. Let's start implementing Redux now. This is important because we want to use the data passed from the server into different pages/components, and a centralized store would help us in that.

Setting up Redux + Next.js

First, let's install redux and next-redux-wrapper which would provide Redux.js wrapper for Next.js projects. Install the package on your systems using the following command:

npm install react-redux redux next-redux-wrapper --save

Next, we'll set up our Redux store. Think of how we set up the default state in the case of Context API. This is very similar to those lines. A store is basically a centralized place for all of your components to store their data and retrieve data from that particular area.

Because it is centralized and decoupled from your components, there could be problems reading/writing values to that area;hence, there has to be a streamlined way to access only the values a component needs to read.

Similarly, if you want to write (update) the redux state, you cannot do it directly. You have to write a **reducer** for it, that is, something that reduces your state. Once you write a reducer for your store, you can then write **dispatchers**. These functions are called dispatchers because they dispatch certain actions to these reducers, and these reducers on receiving those actions, update the state accordingly depending on what actions they received. The following diagram shows how Redux architecture works in a nutshell:

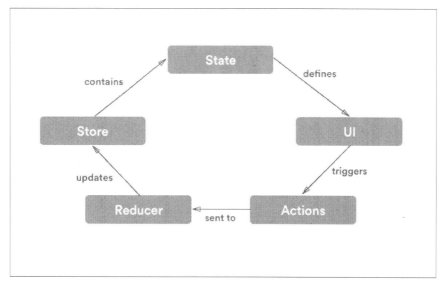

Figure 7.6

If this confusesyou, don't worry. It'll make a lot more sense when we go through this thing again but using code this time. Let's now look at our reducer code:

1. Create a file named reducer.ts in the redux folder located in the project directory (create the redux folder). Here's the reducer code:

```ts
// reducer.ts
type Action = {
  type: string
  payload?: any
}
export type UserDetails = {
  name: string
  age: number
  favQuote: string
```

```
}
export type State = {
 user: UserDetails | null
}
const defaultState: State = {
 user: null
}
const reducer = (state: State = defaultState, action: Action) => {
 switch (action.type) {
    case 'SET_USER_DETAILS':
      return {
    ...state,
    user: <UserDetails>action.payload
  }
    default:
      return state
  }
}
export default reducer
```

Here, you could see that we're creating a Redux store and reducer. A store, as described above, is a place to store data, whereas a reducer is a function that uses certain dispatched actions to update the store. Let's learn about how this code is working:

- First, we defined some types ofTypeScript.

- Then we created a reducer function.

- The reducer function takes two arguments, the first one is the actual application state, which is populated by redux automatically before the reducer is called by redux.

- The second argument is the action. Our task is just to dispatch these actions via dispatcher functions. Redux automatically calls the reducer function.

- This action is actually an object, which consists of a type and payload.

- The type of property defines what this action is supposed to update.

- The payload property is some additional data you can transfer to the reducer to update the state.

This is how the file structure looks like:

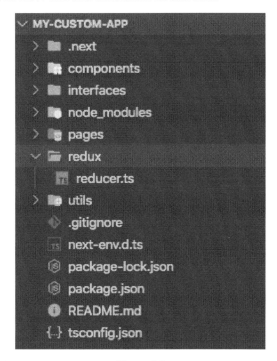

Figure 7.7

The preceding screenshot shows how the file structure looks right now.

2. Once that is done, now we have to integrate Redux in our app. We use the special pages/_app.js (or actually, _app.tsx) file to do that. Let's discuss that now.

_app.js File

According to the documentation:

- Next.js uses the App component to initialize pages

- To override, create the ./pages/_app.js file and override the App class

Basically, this file allows you to override some default configuration Next.js uses to serve the pages. Since we want Redux to be available everywhere on every page, we can wrap the Redux's Provider (just like we wrapped the Context API provider) in this particular file.

Because we're using TypeScript, we'll be creating a file called _app.tsx file instead. Let's go ahead and create it:

```
// pages/_app.tsx
import React from 'react'
import { createStore, Store, compose } from 'redux'
import { Provider } from 'react-redux'
import withRedux from 'next-redux-wrapper'
import reducer, { State } from '../redux/reducer'
import { NextPage } from 'next'
import { NextComponentType, NextPageContext } from 'next/dist/next-server/
lib/utils'
let devTools = (f: any) => f
if(process.browser) {
  const _window = window as any
  if(_window.__REDUX_DEVTOOLS_EXTENSION__) {
devTools = _window.__REDUX_DEVTOOLS_EXTENSION__()
  }
}
const makeStore = (initialState: State) => {
    return createStore(reducer, initialState, compose(devTools))
}
type Props = {
  Component: NextComponentType<NextPageContext>,
pageProps: any,
  store: Store
}
```

```
const MyApp: NextPage<Props> = props => {

 const { Component, pageProps, store } = props

 return (

<Provider store={store}>

<Component {...pageProps} />

</Provider>

 )

}

export default withRedux(makeStore)(MyApp)
```

Let's go over what's happening in this file:

- We import createStore and Store from the redux package. The storeis an interface for the store we'll use.

- We get withRedux**Higher Order Component** (HOC).

- We then register for redux devtools to work correctly. For this, you must have Redux DevTools chrome extension installed in your browser. You can find it for free on extension store

- Then we write our file like a normal next page with typed props.

- See where we destructure the Component, pageProps, and store from the props of MyApp? That's because this file is run by Next.js before every page is sent and you could modify that before that is rendered (or sent).

- We just wrap our original Component which was supposed to be sent in the Provider component provided by the react-redux package.

- The package next-redux-wrapper under the hood initializes the store both on the client and server and handles the technical part.

At this point, if you see your application and download the Redux DevTools extension for Chrome, in your Chrome DevTools, you should see that Redux is working and you should get an empty redux user store:

Figure 7.8

The preceding screenshot shows our integration of Redux in the app.

With that done, let's move back to our app logic and use Redux in it. You can see redux uses the name of our reducer (i.e. user in this case) as the name of the store as well.

Dispatching Redux Actions

In order to change the state in the Redux store, we need to dispatch actions. Actions inform redux that there is a change in conditions and state should be modified somehow. However, it is not necessary that a dispatch should always update the state. Let's create a new file called redux/actions.ts which would have the following code:

```
import { UserDetails } from './reducer'

export const setUserDetails = (payload: UserDetails) => {

  return { type: 'SET_USER_DETAILS', payload }

}
```

And now, we would use this action in our root page. Let's update pages/index.tsx to the following:

```
import React, { useState } from 'react'

import { NextPage } from 'next'

import './styles.css'

import { connect } from 'react-redux'
```

```
import { setUserDetails } from '../redux/actions'
type Props = {
setUserDetails(json: any): void
name?: string
}
const IndexPage: NextPage<Props> = (props) => {
 const [username, setUsername] = useState<string>('')
 const [password, setPassword] = useState<string>('')
 async function submitForm() {
  const req = await fetch('/api/login', {
   method: 'POST',
   headers: {
    'Content-Type': 'application/json'
   },
   body: JSON.stringify({ username, password })
  })
  const json = await req.json()
  console.log(json)
props.setUserDetails(json.data)
 }
 return (
<form method="POST">
<div className="box">
<h1>Login</h1>
    {props.name || 'na'}
<input type="text" placeholder="Username" className="field"
value={username} onChange={e =>setUsername(e.target.value)} />

<input type="password" placeholder="Password" className="field"
value={password} onChange={e =>setPassword(e.target.value)} />

<div className="btn" onClick={submitForm}>Sign In</div>
</div>
</form>
```

```
 )
}
const mapStateToProps = ({ user }: any) => {
  return {
    name: user && user.name
  }
}
```

export default connect(mapStateToProps, { setUserDetails })(IndexPage)

So, what's going on in this file? Let's see:

- We imported the action function, which we just created.

- When we login, we now call a function which we are receiving somehow as the component props. How? We'll see.

- Then we create something called mapStateToProps. For redux, we can extract certain values we want from our central store. Remember the name of our reducer was user? We destruct (ES6 destruction) the user reducer and try to extract the name property if it is available.

- We finally exported the component, not as IndexPage but wrapped inside an HoC. The first argument is the mapStateToProps we created. The second argument is the methods we pass, which would be available in our props. When you call these methods, the return value from these methods is dispatched to the redux store. Now, one of the reducers would capture that action (using its type) and update the state accordingly.

You would see now, that when we login using the correct credentials (admin and admin as the username and password), we would see our name replaced in the login form, and if you check the Redux DevTools, you'll see an appropriate action dispatched against it as well, which would update the redux state:

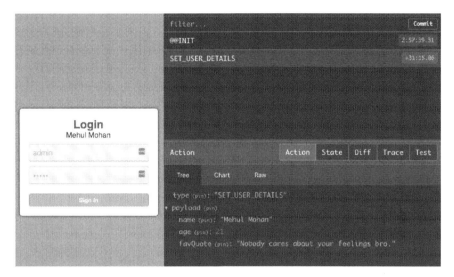

Figure 7.9

The preceding screenshot shows correctly dispatching an action to our Redux store.

But there's something more we can do, even to this page! When React introduced hooks, redux shortly brought in hooks support as well! So, instead of using the connect function to connect the central store with components, we can bring the values we need from the store using the provided redux hooks directly.

Similarly, if we want to dispatch actions, we can dispatch them too using a dispatcher redux provides us, through a hook. Let's change our above file to make use of hooks instead.

useSelector and useDispatch

These two hooks allow us to make use of Redux with hooks in React (pretty much how you'd use useContext). Let's see how above file could be written in hooks:

import React, { useState } from 'react'

import { NextPage } from 'next'

import './styles.css'

import { useSelector, useDispatch } from 'react-redux'

```
import { setUserDetails } from '../redux/actions'
const IndexPage: NextPage = () => {
  const dispatch = useDispatch()
  const name = useSelector((state: any) =>state.user&& state.user.name)
  const [username, setUsername] = useState<string>('')
  const [password, setPassword] = useState<string>('')
  async function submitForm() {
    const req = await fetch('/api/login', {
      method: 'POST',
      headers: {
        'Content-Type': 'application/json'
      },
      body: JSON.stringify({ username, password })
    })
    const json = await req.json()
    console.log(json)
    dispatch(setUserDetails(json.data))
  }
  return (
<form method="POST">
<div className="box">
<h1>Login</h1>
    {name || 'na'}
<input type="text" placeholder="Username" className="field"
value={username} onChange={e =>setUsername(e.target.value)} />
<input type="password" placeholder="Password" className="field"
value={password} onChange={e =>setPassword(e.target.value)} />
<div className="btn" onClick={submitForm}>Sign In</div>
</div>
</form>
```

```
 )
}
```

export default IndexPage

Here's what's happening:

- Clearly, we can see that this code looks much concise and cleaner than the above, plus we avoid the extra component hierarchy when we don't use an HoC above our main component.

- useDispatch() hook just returns us a dispatch function which we have to wrap around our dispatch methods. Remember, the function setUserDetails actually returns a plain object, and we're actually calling dispatch with the first argument as a plain JSON object only. The reason we didn't need to call dispatch earlier was because that was done by redux under the hood when we passed it in the connect method.

- useSelector() hook allows you to pass a function that allows you to filter out which value you want to extract out. useSelector() performs a shallow comparison by default on change and would re-render the component if that shallow comparison detects any change. For our case right now, our user object changes from null to a well-defined object, so it should be fine for us.

Now if we look at the output, there should be no difference whatsoever, and it should just work fine. This is how we would use hooks with React + Redux.

Creating the Dashboard page

Let's go ahead and create a dashboard page with a dashboard/index. tsx file in pages/ directory. Here's how the file structure would look like:

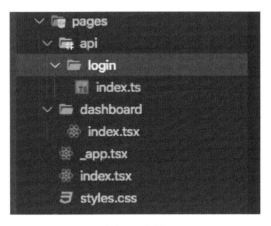

Figure 7.10

The preceding screenshot shows how the file structure looks right now.

We'll keep our dashboard page simple for now, and would just put the following code in the dashboard/index.tsx file:

```
import React from 'react'
import { NextPage } from 'next'
import { useSelector } from 'react-redux'
const DashboardPage: NextPage = () => {
  const user = useSelector((state: any) =>state.user)
  if(!user) return <p>User not available</p>
  return (
<div id="dashboard">
<h1>Hello {user.name}</h1>
<p>Your favorite quote: {user.favQuote}</p>
</div>
  )
}
export default DashboardPage
```

Alright! Now it's time to redirect the user to /dashboard route only when the login was correct. Let's update our pages/index.tsx file.

Conditional routing

To conditionally redirect the user to a different page, we'll use the Router package from next/router. Let's go ahead and use it:

```tsx
// pages/index.tsx

import React, { useState } from 'react'

import { NextPage } from 'next'

import './styles.css'

import { useSelector, useDispatch } from 'react-redux'

import { setUserDetails } from '../redux/actions'

import Router from 'next/router'

const IndexPage: NextPage = () => {

  const dispatch = useDispatch()

  const name = useSelector((state: any) =>state.user&& state.user.name)

  const [username, setUsername] = useState<string>('')

  const [password, setPassword] = useState<string>('')

  async function submitForm() {

    const req = await fetch('/api/login', {

      method: 'POST',

      headers: {

        'Content-Type': 'application/json'

      },

      body: JSON.stringify({ username, password })

    })

    const json = await req.json()

    if(json.status === 'ok') {

      dispatch(setUserDetails(json.data))

Router.push('/dashboard')

    } else {

      alert('Incorrect Login')

    }

  }
```

```
 return (

<form method="POST">

<div className="box">

<h1>Login</h1>

    {name || 'na'}

<input type="text" placeholder="Username" className="field"
value={username} onChange={e =>setUsername(e.target.value)} />

<input type="password" placeholder="Password" className="field"
value={password} onChange={e =>setPassword(e.target.value)} />

<div className="btn" onClick={submitForm}>Sign In</div>

</div>

</form>

 )

}
export default IndexPage
```

Now when you hit login with correct credentials, you should get something like this:

Figure 7.12

The preceding screenshot shows what the Dashboard page would look like.

And when you refresh the page, you should get the message **User not found**, which is correct by logic, as we're not persisting our redux store, nor are we trying to see if the user is already logged in the application and if yes, retrieve the user data. We'll fix that later.

Let's look at nested routing first.

Nested routes

Let's start with a simple use case. We've created top-level paths (that is,/home or /about, and so on) but how about /home/page-x? Well, it turns out that in Next.js it is as simple as nesting folders inside one another. Let's create the following file:

pages/path1/path2/path3.tsx

And write the following code inside it:

```
import React from 'react'

import { NextPage } from 'next'

const PathPage: NextPage = () => {

  return (

<h1>Hello from very deep inside!</h1>

  )

}

export default PathPage
```

Let the server apply changes, and when you visit http://localhost:3000/path1/path2/path3, you should be able to see the following:

Figure 7.13

The preceding screenshot shows an example of nesting routing in the browser.

Another thing you should know about is that you can create path3 as the folder and place the preceding code in path3/index.tsx and it would work just the same. With Next.js 9+, we also have support for dynamic routing. Let's see what it is and how it can work.

Dynamic routing

Next.js has recently introduced dynamic routing, which opens doors for matching a whole lot of URLs instead of just static routes which we've been doing so far with the pages directory. Let's create a file called users/index.tsx inside the pages/ directory. We would also create a file called users/[param].tsx. Here's the code for both:

```
// pages/users/index.tsx
import React from 'react'
import { NextPage } from 'next'
const UsersPage: NextPage = () => {
  return (
<h1>Just a regular file</h1>
  )
}
export default UsersPage
```

And the other file:

```
// pages/users/[param].tsx
import React from 'react'
import { NextPage } from 'next'
const UsersPageDynamic: NextPage = () => {
  return (
<h1>Just a regular file too</h1>
  )
}
export default UsersPageDynamic
```

Now, when you visit http://localhost:3000/users, you'll see this page:

Figure 7.14

But if you visit any other route matching /users/<anything here> you'll
see this:

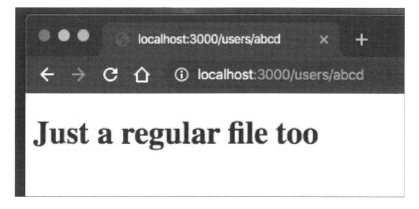

Figure 7.15

But we know that we don't have any file named users/abcd. So, what's
happening here?

- When you name a file in square brackets (like we did with
  [param].tsx), that means Next.js considers it to match anything
  when placed under a different route.

- Then what about the name of the file? Well, we can extract
  information about the route using the param, that is, the
  name of the file. Let's modify our [param].tsx file to better
  reflect this:

  // pages/users/[param].tsx

  import React from 'react'

```
import { NextPage } from 'next'

import { useRouter } from 'next/router'

const UsersPageDynamic: NextPage = () => {

 const router = useRouter()

 console.log(router)

 return (

<h1>Just a regular file too {router.query.param}</h1>

 )

}

export default UsersPageDynamic
```

With this being there, if I visit the URL http://localhost:3000/users/mehul I should see the following in the console:

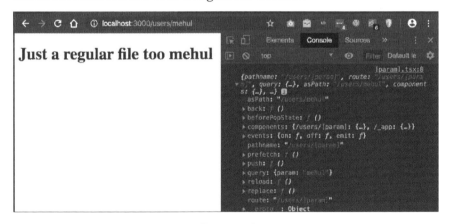

Figure 7.16

Let's discuss why that is the case:

- You can see, in the URL the param value is mehul which is reflected on the screen because of router.query.param

- On the right, in the console, we can get all the information the hook useRouter returns us. We can see param is one of them inside the query property. This is coming directly from the name of the file. If you name the file something else, it would be something else.

Okay. Now that we know about dynamic routing, it'll be easier for us to handle use cases like creating social media like a website where you can access anyone's profile within the URL. Let's now go ahead and implement a quick registration page as well in our app.

Registration page

Let's create a path /register using Next.js:

```
// pages/register/index.tsx
import React, { useState } from 'react'
import { NextPage } from 'next'
import './styles.css'
import { useDispatch } from 'react-redux'
import { setUserDetails } from '../../redux/actions'
import Router from 'next/router'
const RegisterPage: NextPage = () => {
 const dispatch = useDispatch()
 const [username, setUsername] = useState<string>('')
 const [password, setPassword] = useState<string>('')
 const [name, setName] = useState<string>('')
 const [age, setAge] = useState<string>('')
 const [quote, setQuote] = useState<string>('')
 async function submitForm() {
  const req = await fetch('/api/register', {
    method: 'POST',
    headers: {
     'Content-Type': 'application/json'
    },
    body: JSON.stringify({ username, password, name, age, quote })
  })
  const json = await req.json()
  if(json.status === 'ok') {
   dispatch(setUserDetails(json.data))
Router.push('/dashboard')
```

```
  } else {
    alert('Error Registering')
  }
}
return (
<form method="POST">
<div className="box">
<h1>Register</h1>
<input type="text" placeholder="Username" className="field"
value={username} onChange={e =>setUsername(e.target.value)} />

<input type="text" placeholder="Name" className="field" value={name}
onChange={e =>setName(e.target.value)} />

<input type="text" placeholder="Age" className="field" value={age}
onChange={e =>setAge(e.target.value)} />

<input type="text" placeholder="Fav. Quote" className="field" value={quote}
onChange={e =>setQuote(e.target.value)} />

<input type="password" placeholder="Password" className="field"
value={password} onChange={e =>setPassword(e.target.value)} />

<div className="btn" onClick={submitForm}>Register</div>
</div>
</form>
 )
}
export default RegisterPage
```

Here, we just get all the required information we need from the user and send it to our API backend.

And we'll just copy-paste the styles from IndexPage itself:

```
// pages/register/styles.css
* {
  margin: 0;
  padding: 0;
  box-sizing: border-box;
```

```
    outline: 0;
}
body {
  font-family: 'Open Sans', sans-serif;
  background: #3498db;
  margin: 0 auto 0 auto;
  width: 100%;
  text-align: center;
  margin: 20px 0px 20px 0px;
}
p {
  font-size: 12px;
  text-decoration: none;
  color: #ffffff;
}
h1 {
  font-size: 1.5em;
  color: #525252;
}
.box {
  background: white;
  width: 300px;
  position: absolute;
  top: 50%;
  left: 50%;
  transform: translate(-50%, -50%);
  border-radius: 6px;
  padding: 20px;
  box-shadow: 0 0 5px black;
}
.field {
```

```css
  background: #ecf0f1;
  border: #ccc 1px solid;
  border-bottom: #ccc 2px solid;
  padding: 8px;
  width: 100%;
  color: #AAA;
  margin-top: 10px;
  font-size: 1em;
  border-radius: 4px;
}
.btn {
  background: #2ecc71;
  width: 100%;
  cursor: pointer;
  padding: 5px 0;
  color: white;
  border-radius: 4px;
  border: #27ae60 1px solid;
  margin-top: 20px;
  font-weight: 800;
  font-size: 0.8em;
}
.btn:hover {
  background: #2CC06B;
}
```

Let's create our api/register endpoint now:

```ts
// api/register/index.ts
import { NextApiRequest, NextApiResponse } from 'next'
import methods from './userlist'
export default async (req: NextApiRequest, rcs: NextApiResponse) => {
```

```
const { username, password, name, age, favQuote } = req.body
if(!methods.doesUserExist(username)) {
methods.addUser(username, password, { name, age, favQuote })
  return res.json({ status: 'ok', data: { name, age, favQuote } })
  } else {
  return res.json({ status: 'error', message: 'User already registered' })

  }

}
```

Here, you can see that I'm making use of a file called userlist.ts and calling some utility functions through it. This would technically be a database on a real site, but for simplicity, we can have an in-memory data structure (a JS object) to store our registrations temporarily.

Here's how the userlist.ts file would look like:

```
type DataType = {
  name: string
  age: string
favQuote: string
}
type UserType = {
  username: string
  password: string
  data: DataType
}
const users: UserType[] = []
const methods = {
getUsers(): UserType[] {
  return users
  },
doesUserExist(username: string): boolean {
  return !!users.find(user =>user.username === username)
  },
```

```
addUser(username: string, password: string, data: DataType) {
users.push({ username, password, data })

  return true

 }

}
export default methods
```

This file is pretty much self-explanatory. We are exposing a bunch of methods to operate on a dynamic user list we are maintaining in the user array. Since Node exports are singletons (that is, multiple imports to the same file refer to the same object/array in memory), we can expect this to be consistent.

Alright! Now we can go ahead and register some accounts on the frontend with their custom quotes! As an assignment, try to complete this app even more by including authentication checks and data fetching on all pages if the user is logged in.

Conclusion

In this chapter, we spent the much-needed time we needed to spend in the Next.js ecosystem. We also looked at Redux in-depth, setting up redux with Next.js, routing with Next and how to spin APIs without getting out of Next.js framework. We now have a good amount of knowledge to create basic to intermediate complex server-side rendered backends with Next.js. In the next chapter, we'll learn more about what we could achieve with the React technology, in the field of Progressive Web Apps.

Questions

1. What is the difference between TypeScript and JavaScript? Is all valid JavaScript valid TypeScript too?

2. What is Redux? How does it work?

3. What does getInitialProps do in Next.js?

4. What is the difference between the pages folder and the api folder in Next.js?

5. What do you mean by reducer in Redux?

6. What does the _app.js file do? There is another such file called _document.js in Next.js. Can you find what it does?

7. What is the difference between nested and dynamic routing? Can dynamic routes be nested with Next v9.x?

CHAPTER 8

Progressive Web Apps

In the last chapter, we learned about Next.js technology and how it is powering the SSR world of React today. When web apps meet native apps, a different type of application is born, which is Progressive Web App. We'll learn all about PWAs in this chapter and see how to create one using React as our primary frontend library.

Structure

- What is **Progressive Web App (PWA)**
- Getting started with PWA
- manifest.json File
- Service workers
- PWA using Next.js
- Custom server with Next.js

Objective

In this chapter, our main aim would be to understand what progressive web apps are and how to set them up with our React and Next.js projects. Along the way, we'll learn more about these technologies.

What is a progressive web app?

A progressive web app is a web app eventually, but a bit better. It uses modern web features to deliver great user experience, similar to the one you'll experience using a native app. Some features of a progressive web app:

1. Responsive: Obviously, your app should be fit for all screens and sizes, and fortunately, these days creating a responsive site (or converting an existing site to responsive design) is not very hard unless the code is very old.

2. Independent of the internet: Your PWA would be working with something called service workers (more on this later) which enables them to work offline or on low-speed internet connections.

3. HTTPS: PWA works on HTTPS only.

4. Installable: Your PWA can be installed as a regular app on phones (and as a chrome browser app).

5. Linkable: Can be shared with a simple URL

Hello World

Let's create a new React project with create-react-app and start implementing our PWA. We'll start with a simple way using TypeScript:

```
create-react-app pwa-app --typescript
```

Once it's ready, we'll see a file structure something like this:

Figure 8.1

Let's look at the following bolded lines in our src/index.tsx file:

import React from 'react';

import ReactDOM from 'react-dom';

import './index.css';

import App from './App';

import * as serviceWorker from './serviceWorker';

ReactDOM.render(<App />, document.getElementById('root'));

// If you want your app to work offline and load faster, you can change

// unregister() to register() below. Note this comes with some pitfalls.

// Learn more about service workers: https://bit.ly/CRA-PWA

serviceWorker.unregister();

We're importing a file we're calling serviceWorker. We'll come to what service workers are shortly, but for now, let's change the unregister method call to register and build the app using:

npm run build

This would create a build folder in your project's root directory. Now, run a simple local development server inside this directory. This depends on what dependencies you have installed. If you have python installed (installed by default on macOS and Linux), run the following command inside the build folder:

python -m SimpleHTTPServer 1234 # for python 2

If you're using python3, use the following bash command:

python3 -m http.server 1234

If you have PHP command line installed, you can also start a local development server by:

php -S localhost:1234

Make sure to run all these commands when you're inside the build folder on the command line as they'll serve as the root directory of http://localhost:1234.

Now, let's go ahead and visit the site localhost:1234. Nothing too strange, except for two things. If we look at the **Network Requests** tab in Chrome DevTools, we'll see some special files being requested which have a gear icon in front of them (known as service workers):

⚙ service-worker.js	200	javascript	Other
⚙ workbox-sw.js	200	javascript	service-worker.js:14
⚙ precache-manifest.01aeacade56ec22296...	200	javascript	service-worker.js:16
⚙ workbox-core.dev.js	200	javascript	WorkboxSW.mjs:111
⚙ workbox-precaching.dev.js	200	javascript	WorkboxSW.mjs:111
⚙ workbox-routing.dev.js	200	javascript	WorkboxSW.mjs:111

Figure 8.2

And the other thing is we see a little add icon (+) in Chrome's Omnibox:

Figure 8.3

Clicking on that reveals a dialog box prompting to add this application to chrome as if we're installing some sort of application to our browser! Let's add this:

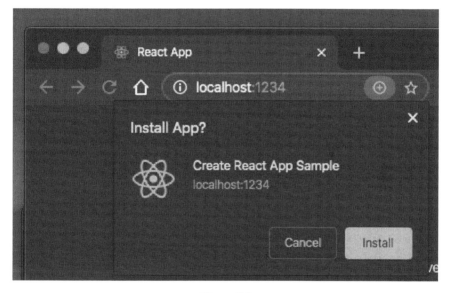

Figure 8.4

Once we install the app, it is a standalone application that you can see in the Chrome Apps folder. Double-clicking on the app actually opens a separate window in which we see our same app, but this time, it feels like we're running an actual desktop application, not a website or a web URL. This is a very basic example of a progressive web app.

Now although we're running this on localhost, if you deploy this website somewhere online (HTTPSrequired), and add the app just like we did,usingthe (+) icon, you'll see that your app would work even without internet! We'll see how this happens soon and would look more into PWAs now:

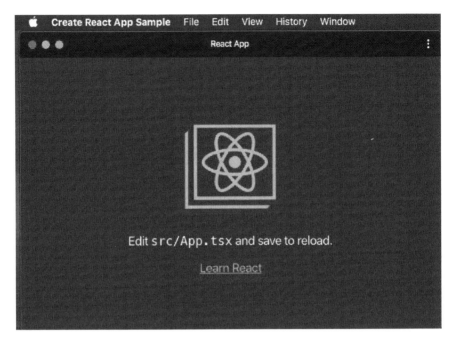

Figure 8.5

manifest.json file

In the public folder, there is a file called manifest.json, which is a simple JSON file describing some properties of our installed PWA. You can see that we include this manifest.json in our index.html file using the following line of code:

```
<link rel="manifest" href="%PUBLIC_URL%/manifest.json" />
```

And the manifest.json file looks like the following:

```
{
  "short_name": "React App",
  "name": "Create React App Sample",
  "icons": [
    {
      "src": "favicon.ico",
      "sizes": "64x64 32x32 24x24 16x16",
      "type": "image/x-icon"
```

```
  },
  {
    "src": "logo192.png",
    "type": "image/png",
    "sizes": "192x192"
  },
  {
    "src": "logo512.png",
    "type": "image/png",
    "sizes": "512x512"
  }
],
"start_url": ".",
"display": "standalone",
"theme_color": "#000000",
"background_color": "#ffffff"
}
```

Let's go on these properties quickly:

- short_name/name: These are used for naming your application. At least one of them must be specified (you can specify both). If you specify both, short_name would be used in places with limited space, like the toolbar (you can see above in the screenshot, the toolbar holds the title React App and not Create React App Sample).

- icons: As the prop name says, these are the icons used for your application and what the end-user sees.

- start_url: This URL is the URL where your app should start when it is launched. Usually, you'll just want to keep it to your root URL, or you can pass in some query parameters to track when your app is opened. For example, passing /?utm_source=app_opened would allow you to track how many times your PWA is opened.

- display: This allows you to set how your app should be launched. Because PWA is a web app anyway, it's launched inside a browser instance only. Here are the values and what they do:

value	Description
fullscreen	Opens the app in fullscreen mode
standalone	Opens the app in a native-looking app window
minimal-ui	Similar to fullscreen, but provides more UI elements for controlling navigation
browser	Opens your URL in the browser

If you want the Add to Home Screen Prompt we just saw above, your display value should be set to standalone only:

- theme_color: This is the color of the toolbar of the application.

- background_color: This is the splash screen background color (for mobile phones) when the app is launched.

You can, in fact, generate your own manifest.json file easily using online tools like https://app-manifest.firebaseapp.com/.

Service workers

Think of a service worker as a JavaScript file sitting between your application and the network layer. That means, whenever your browser tries to connect to the network (URL owned by you), that passes through a service worker file. Similarly, when there's a response back from the network (your server), that goes through the service worker before it is received by your app.

One important thing to note is that service workers, just like web workers, run in a separate thread (that doesn't mean that JS is multithreaded), so your UI is never blocked.

Lifecycle

Here's a good image showing how service workers' lifecycle looks like:

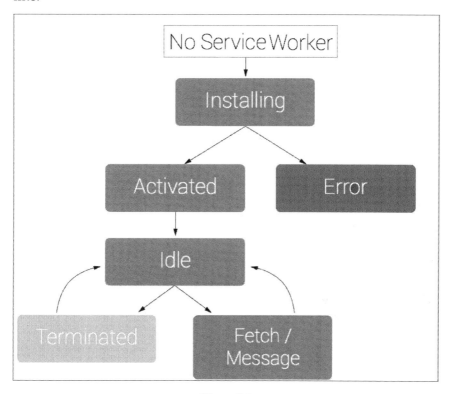

Figure 8.6

In our case, once the service worker is activated, it starts fetching static resources and starts caching them for local/offline use.

Let's look at our build folder. In the build folder, we have a file called service-worker.js, which imports the following twoscripts at the top:

```
importScripts("https://storage.googleapis.com/workbox-cdn/releases/4.3.1/
workbox-sw.js");

importScripts(

  "/precache-manifest.01aeacade56ec22296e752a5407421fc.js"

);
```

The first script is a Workbox script. Workbox is a set of JavaScript libraries built by Google over the existing raw PWA API to provide flexible methods and ways to implement features like caching in your PWA and eliminates a lot of boilerplate.

The second script, is a create-react-app generated file, and if you open it, you'll see it consists of static resources (HTML files, CSS files, JavaScript files and images) your app is using with their absolute URL paths. Finally, at the last, the service-worker.js file contains the following snippet:

```
self.__precacheManifest = [].concat(self.__precacheManifest || []);

workbox.precaching.precacheAndRoute(self.__precacheManifest, {});

workbox.routing.registerNavigationRoute(workbox.precaching.
getCacheKeyForURL("/index.html"), {

  blacklist: [/^\/_/,/\/[^\/?]+\.[^\/]+$/],

});
```

In short, this script registers all the routes described in our precache-manifest file to the service worker and tells them to cache these resources. Since React applications are effectively **Single Page Applications** (**SPA**), we use the registerNavigationRoute method of the workbox.routing API to send our index.html file on any route hit our app receives from the user. This allows React to take control of the routing system again and do the needful internal routing using react-router or whatever implementation is present.

PWA using Next.js

Now that we have a decent understanding of what a PWA is and how it works basically let's shift our focus to how we can implement PWA using Next.js.

Let's start by creating a simple Next.js project. You can setup Next.js manually as we did in the last chapters, or we can just make use of a handy create-next-app utility like this to do the same:

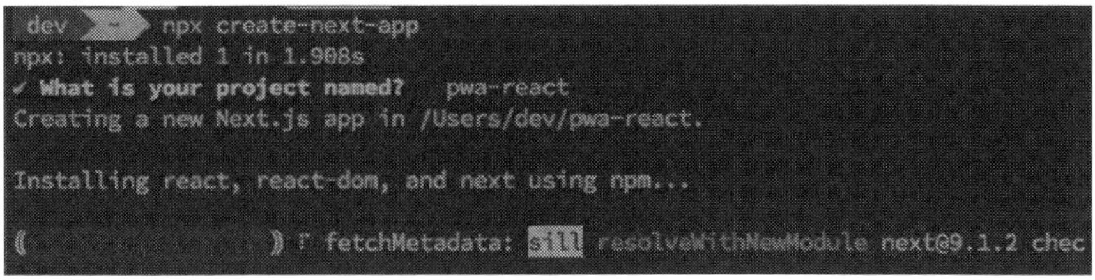

Figure 8.7

This would basically initialize our setup in the same way we did before. Once that is done, we need to install another package called next-offline. This would enable service worker support for our app and eventually support for PWA.

npm install --save next-offline

This would install the next-offline package. Once that is done, create a new file called next.config.js in the project, and this is what would go inside that file:

```
// next.config.js

constwithOffline = require('next-offline')

constnextConfig = {}

module.exports = withOffline(nextConfig)
```

There is a lot of default configuration which the next-offline package uses, and by default, we can safely stick to it. Basically, what the withOffline function would do, is that it would inject a service worker script with the passed options when the bundle for Next.js is prepared. Let's build our next project using npm run build. In the build folder, we'll see that in the main-<hash>.js file, you'll see the following compressed snippet somewhere:

```
navigator.serviceWorker.register("/service-worker.js",{scope:"/"}).then....
```

Now, just like we did with the above react app, we need to serve our service-worker.js file. Don't worry, and we don't have to code it ourselves as it is again, created by Next automatically! But we surely need to serve it on /service-worker.js URL, and you know, in Next, static files are served under the static directory.

Now, although we can move our service worker file in the static directory and change the path of service worker using the configuration above, we'll go ahead and try to redirect all requests coming to /service-worker.js to the file on our filesystem and let Next handle rest of the requests by creating a custom server.

Custom Next.js Server

Create a file called server.js in the root of project and write the following contents inside it:

```
const { createServer } = require('http')

const { join } = require('path')

const { parse } = require('url')

const next = require('next')

const app = next({ dev: process.env.NODE_ENV !== 'production' })

const handle = app.getRequestHandler()

app.prepare()
 .then(() => {
createServer((req, res) => {
constparsedUrl = parse(req.url, true)
const { pathname } = parsedUrl
    // handle GET request to /service-worker.js
    if (pathname === '/service-worker.js') {
constfilePath = join(__dirname, '.next', pathname)
app.serveStatic(req, res, filePath)
    } else {
      handle(req, res, parsedUrl)
    }
  })
  .listen(3000, () => {
    console.log(`> Ready on http://localhost:${3000}`)
  })
})
```

This code is directly picked from official Next docs, but let's go over what is happening here:

- Because this script is directly executed by node, it doesn't pass through webpack or babel, so you have to use CommonJS imports here.

- Then we bring in the Node's `createServer` method from the http package to create a custom server.

- We also import the package next. Here's how the next API works.

next(config: object)

The config object consists of the following:

- dev: A Boolean indicating the development/production mode (default: false)

- dir: Location where the project is present (default: '.')

- quiet: Whether to hide error messages containing server info (default: false)

- conf: Next.js configuration object (same object which is read from next.config.js file)

This returns us the app object, which has a bunch of methods associated with it for custom routing. We'll only look at `getRequestHandler` and `serveStatic` though.

getRequestHandler()

This method basically allows Next to handle routing just like default way, so in essence, when we don't want our custom logic to take place, we'll call this method with the appropriate req and res objects from the `createServer` method.

It returns us another function, `handle`, which can be called using the request and response objects coming from our server.

serveStatic()

We use another package called url to parse the URL into different parts—hostname, pathname, protocol, port, and so on.

Finally, we check, if the pathname actually matches /service-worker.js. If yes, we use the `app.serveStatic()` method. Basically, we pass in the req and res objects with the path where to resolve the static asset to. In our case, our file service-worker.js is present inside the .next folder as a direct child, so we just use path.join to get the path directly.

Once that is done, we'll need to make a bunch of changes to our package.json file too. Your scripts section inside the JSON file should look like this:

```
"scripts": {
    "dev": "node server.js",
    "build": "next build",
    "start": "NODE_ENV=production node server.js"
}
```

Finally, let's create a manifest.json file similar to last time and place it in the .next folder and add a custom route for it. So the manifest.json file would look like:

```
{
  "short_name": "React App",
  "name": "Create React App Sample",
  "icons": [
    {
      "src": "favicon.ico",
      "sizes": "64x64 32x32 24x24 16x16",
      "type": "image/x-icon"
    },
    {
      "src": "logo192.png",
      "type": "image/png",
      "sizes": "192x192"
    },
    {
      "src": "logo512.png",
      "type": "image/png",
      "sizes": "512x512"
```

```
  }
  ],
  "start_url": ".",
  "display": "standalone",
  "theme_color": "#000000",
  "background_color": "#ffffff"
}
```

And our server.js file would look like:

```
const { createServer } = require('http')

const { join } = require('path')

const { parse } = require('url')

const next = require('next')

const app = next({ dev: process.env.NODE_ENV !== 'production' })

const handle = app.getRequestHandler()

app.prepare()

.then(() => {

createServer((req, res) => {

constparsedUrl = parse(req.url, true)

const { pathname } = parsedUrl

// handle GET request to /service-worker.js

if (pathname === '/service-worker.js' || pathname === '/manifest.json' ||
pathname === '/logo512.png' || pathname === '/logo192.png') {

constfilePath = join(__dirname, '.next', pathname)

app.serveStatic(req, res, filePath)

} else {

handle(req, res, parsedUrl)

}

})

.listen(3000, () => {

console.log(`> Ready on http://localhost:${3000}`)

})
```

})

Don't forget to place your icons as well in the .next folder! Finally, to serve our manifest.json file, we need to include it as a link tag in every page (just like we did with React example above). Let's do that using the _document.js file in Next.js.

_document.js

This file inside the pages folder allows us to inject our custom markup in various places (like the head of the page). We'll use the following file to inject the manifest.json:

```
// pages/_document.js

import Document, { Html, Head, Main, NextScript } from 'next/document'

class MyDocument extends Document {

static async getInitialProps(ctx) {

constinitialProps = await Document.getInitialProps(ctx)

return { ...initialProps }

}

render() {

return (

<Html>

<Head>

<link rel="manifest" href="/manifest.json" />

</Head>

<body>

<Main />

<NextScript />

</body>

</Html>

)

}

}

export default MyDocument
```

And that's it! Here's how the final file structure would look like:

Figure 8.8

Now we can go ahead and run npm run build and npm start to start production build of the app. Once we do, you'll see that you get an option to install PWA now:

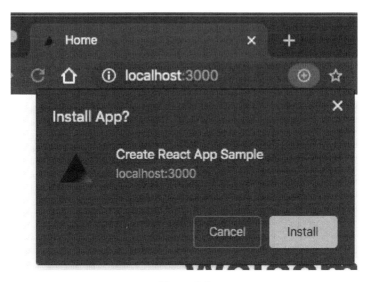

Figure 8.9

Also, on phones, we get the same experience:

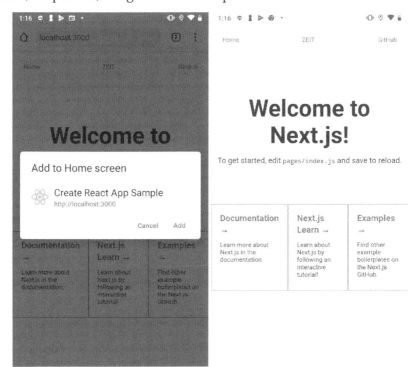

Figure 8.10

Conclusion

In this chapter, we learned about progressive web apps and how to make our React and Next apps progressive. We also saw how to set up a custom Next.js server in the process. In the next chapter, we'll be closing with some of the best practices with React and the future of the library as a whole.

Questions

1. What do you mean by a PWA?

2. How is a PWA different from a native app or a hybrid app?

3. What is the difference between a service worker and a web worker?

4. What is the function of the file _document.js in Next.js framework?

5. How does a custom Next.js server differ from a custom API endpoint programmed in Next.js?

CHAPTER 9

Bleeding Edge React

React has come a long way since its launch in 2013. Today, React has one of the biggest developer communities all over the world. React is continuously improving and developing, as we speak. This chapter would cover some of the bleeding edge features of React, which are either still in the works or are in very experimental stages right now in the React framework, and is definitely going to shape the future of the framework, and the community as a whole. Let's dive into it!

Structure

- How React works
  - ▶ Reconciler
  - ▶ Renderer
- Concurrent Mode
- How concurrent mode works
- Opt-in concurrent mode
- React Suspense

Objective

In the final chapter, we'll see some things React has been working on for the future. The concurrent mode is a big thing, which is experimentally available at the moment for the developers to try out. We'll learn about that in this chapter.

How does React work?

Before diving deep into the fundamentals of the new technology, it's important to make ourselves aware of how React works anyway. On a higher level, React consists of a reconciler and a renderer. A reconciler is a way how React handles the virtual implementation of the DOM tree inside its memory. Let's look at an example first in vDOM.

Reconciler

Virtual DOM is how React maintains a copy of the original DOM the browser shows the end-user, in its own memory. React reconciler handles the creation of this tree in memory only. Note that this tree still doesn't know which environment it is in. For example, when you write the following JSX code:

```
<div className="myClass">
<h1>Hello World</h1>
<p>This is a nice paragraph</p>
</div>
```

This gets transpiled by Babel into the following:

```
React.createElement("div", {
className: "myClass"
}, React.createElement("h1", null, "Hello World"), React.createElement("p", null,
"This is a nice paragraph"));
```

Which is further, gets represented as the following in memory:

```
{
  "type": "div",
```

```
"key": null,
"ref": null,
"props": {
  "className": "myClass",
  "children": [
    {
      "type": "h1",
      "key": null,
      "ref": null,
      "props": {
        "children": "Hello World"
      }
    },
    {
      "type": "p",
      "key": null,
      "ref": null,
      "props": {
        "children": "This is a nice paragraph"
      }
    }
  ]
}
}
```

Note that I've removed some properties from the object above just for clarity. But what we could see previouslyis an object which React has in its memory. This is, in effect, the vDOM. Note that although there is nothing "DOM" here, still, we refer to it as virtual DOM, which is kind of wrong.

Renderer

React's second part is the react renderer. Now, DOM is one of the host environments which could use React. There are other host environments as well, like React Native (for mobile), or maybe React Hardware. Renderers basically allow the reconciler to talk to the host environment.

For example, with DOM, we know that an element is created using document.createElement API exposed by browsers. This might not be the case with a mobile host, say Android. There, you would have to use some other way to create a UI element on the screen, but does it affect the reconciler in any way? No! That is why it is a great decision to split the reconciler and renderer into different packages. When you install react for web pages, you install the package react and react-dom. Here, the package react is basically the reconciler, and the package react-dom is renderer.

Moving from classes

I'm fully aware that React has first-class support for class-based components, but this chapter aims at future tech and experimental tech associated with React, and the team has made it very clear that in the future, functional components would be the ones which would get the most focus on development. With hooks, functional components are fully capable of doing everything class-based components do. If you're just picking up React, I would say just know about class-based components enough to refactor them, but if you're creating your own components, always go with functional components.

Class-based components have their own pros and cons, like, they actually mutate state and props, whereas functional components actually capture the props and state at the time of render. This avoids nasty bugs. Moreover, functional components are a more friendly way to code than classes, simply because JavaScript has no classes;it is just syntactic sugar over functions.

Concurrent mode

The concurrent mode in React is a completely new way of working with React. In Computer Science, concurrency usually means performing multiple tasks on the basis of time slicing. React, once it is done with the vDOM diffs, now has to commit these changes to the DOM. Calculating the changes in vDOM is non-blocking, even now, and it is how internally React works (using browser's idle time by calling requestIdleCallback function in browsers and in different threads for other host environments), however the commit phase, that is, writing to DOM is synchronous. Some notable features of concurrent mode:

1. **Interruptible rendering**: Consider a huge list consisting of items where you could filter for the items. If you ever used such an application, you know that it could become all jittery and lagging unless there is some sort of debounce function in place which doesn't run the search JavaScript logic unless the user has stopped typing (say checking if the last keystroke was 200ms before or so). Concurrent mode fixes this by making the renders interruptible by high priority interrupts. A user interacting with an input field is a higher priority interrupt than react, rendering the updated view, hence, react pauses its execution and frees the main thread to handle the input.

2. **Loading sequences**: Have you ever seen applications where you see the loading spinner just for a split second even though you're on a fast connection? The concurrent mode also solves that problem.

3. **Concurrency**: Last but not least, react can now work truly concurrently, i.e. it can work on multiple state updates simultaneously. This means that if you have some I/O bound data (HTTP network requests) to bring in some data, React can skip over the data for a while and render views. When the data arrives, React can simply place it there. Current standard practice is that we block the whole view from rendering if data is not available.

Concurrent react makes code fetching, data fetching and resource fetching truly concurrent, and if the browser supports, parallel too. As of now, concurrent react is experimental and not stable except for code splitting. So we'll not be using code examples for unstable APIs.

Opting in concurrent mode

The concurrent mode in React is opt-in right now. To use it, instead of:

```
ReactDOM.render(<Component />, container)
```

Use the following:

```
ReactDOM.createRoot(container).render(<Component />)
```

Now you're running React in concurrent mode. This API only exists in the experimental build, and it is very much possible that in the future you might not need this.

Suspense – Code fetching

React comes with Suspense, a component that handles when a part of your application is suspended due to some reason. Basically, Suspense allows your application to wait for something. This "something" could be any async operation - either I/O or memory bound. Let's see how we can make use of that with code. Take a look at the example below:

```
import React from 'react'

constProfilePage = React.lazy(() => import('./ProfilePage')); // Lazy-loaded

// Show a spinner while the profile is loading

<Suspense fallback={<Spinner />}>

<ProfilePage />

</Suspense>
```

Instead of importing the component directly, we wrap it inside React.lazy call. When this component is used, React sees that it is not available and starts a request to fetch the code for this component.

Meanwhile, React also tries to look for a Suspense component as a node in the tree above it and uses the specified fallback component as the placeholder for the same. So, now, as long as ProfilePage is not available and ready, Suspense would show the Spinner in its place.

Suspense – Data fetching

This is where things get interesting. Suspense allows you to fetch data as if you were using data synchronously. This is still experimental, so we'll not be diving deep into the code. Also, make sure to check the updated code if you're reading this book in the future, as the API might have changed. Let's see some code!

```
// This is not a Promise. It's a special object from Suspense integration.
const resource = fetchProfileData();
function ProfilePage() {
  return (
<Suspense fallback={<h1>Loading profile...</h1>}>
<ProfileDetails />
<Suspense fallback={<h1>Loading posts...</h1>}>
<ProfileTimeline />
</Suspense>
</Suspense>
  );
}
function ProfileDetails() {
  // Try to read user info, although it might not have loaded yet
const user = resource.user.read();
  return <h1>{user.name}</h1>;
}
function ProfileTimeline() {
  // Try to read posts, although they might not have loaded yet
const posts = resource.posts.read();
  return (
<ul>
    {posts.map(post => (
<li key={post.id}>{post.text}</li>
    ))}
</ul>
  );
}
```

This code has a lot going on. Let's break it down.

- Firstly, we create a resource. This is special. This is not a Promise or a plain object. This object is created by React which we can use as if we have the data synchronously available with us. If not, React would automatically search the tree for the nearest Suspense component and would let it show the fallback loader. We'll discuss the code for this soon! (The code is highly experimental and is likely to change, so please don't use it in future).

- Then we read from the resource using resource.posts.read(). Notice that this is performed synchronously. Internally, if data is not present, the read() method actually throws under the hood for the Suspense component to catch, and this way, further execution is not performed. In case data is available, it is returned.

- Finally, we use it normally with components.

Let's discuss how the resource is created now. Here's the current unstable implementation of fetchProfileData:

```
import { unstable_createResource } from 'react-cache'

function fetchProfileData() {

return {

  user: unstable_createResource(

    () => fetch('...').then(res =>res.json()) // return a Promise

  ),

  posts: unstable_createResource(

    () => fetch('...').then(res =>res.json()) // return a Promise

  }

}
}
```

Basically, right now, you have to make use of unstable_createResouce which would probably be replaced by just createResource in the future. Here, right now (this might change!) you have to return a Promise which when resolved would make that particular resource available for your React components, and your component would be able to read the return value using resource.read() just like we saw in the earlier example.

Conclusion

In the final chapter of this book, we learned about the upcoming concurrent mode to React and how it would work. I hope this book gave you a base understanding of working with React and Next as a whole and solidified your concepts for React. After all these years working with React, I don't think it is just a UI library, it is a whole development ecosystem, and there's so much more to learn! All the best for your future endeavours.

Questions

1. What is the difference between a reconciler and a renderer? Is react-native a reconciler or a renderer?

2. Class-based components mutate the state and props when they're updated by parent/host, and functional components do not. Find out how functional components work under the hood. (Hint: functional components use hooks which return a new value on every render)

3. How is concurrent mode different from normal React mode?

4. What is the main essence of Suspense? (Hint: waiting for something)

Printed in Great Britain
by Amazon

57374120R00118